Marc

PEOPLE LIKE US

Hodder & Stoughton
LONDON SYDNEY AUCKLAND TORONTO

To Peter Preston

British Library Cataloguing in Publication Data

Marc
People like us
1. English wit and humor, Pictorial
Rn: Mark Boxer I. Title
741.5'942 NC1479

ISBN 0 340 36289 8

 Printed in Great Britain for Hodder and Stoughton Limited, Mill Road, Dunton Green, Sevenoaks, Kent by T. J. Press (Padstow) Ltd., Padstow, Cornwall

Hodder and Stoughton Editorial Office: 47 Bedford Square, London WC1B 3DP

Introduction

When Mrs Thatcher finally makes it to Dulwich what will she be famous for? In the end it may be for a phrase. Harold Macmillan will be largely remembered for 'the Wind of Change' and 'You've never had it so good'. Sir Harold Wilson will be cherished for 'the pound in your pocket' and 'the white heat of technology' and Edward Heath for 'the unacceptable face of capitalism'. (Those who are surprised at Heath coining a memorable phrase at all will be reassured by the recent discovery that he meant to say 'facet' rather than 'face'.)

Mrs Thatcher may well be best remembered for asking 'Is he one of us?'. Though in her case she clearly means a non-wet who believes passionately in privatisation and draconian monetary policies, the words have a distinct echo with the phraseology of pre-war snobbery; 'Not One of Us.' I can remember from my youth similar phrases about a 'little man' or a 'little woman', who usually made curtains for absolutely nothing. I recently heard similar words on the lips of a Tory cabinet minister's wife; she referred to 'little people'. There was no doubt they must be considered, if not actively cared for: her husband is a born-again wet. But the 'them' and 'us' syndrome has never seemed more potent. Mrs Thatcher's legacy will surely be the forging of stronger divisions in English life. The title of the present book reflects the Watford Gap factor.

The cartoons collected here cover the decline in the political fortunes of Margaret Thatcher from 1984 to 1986. They come mainly from the *Guardian* and also from a regular slot in *Private Eye* sponsored by a Vodka firm. Some have not been published before because of the susceptibilities of the client, though one got through which so horrified the parent company that the arrangement sadly came to an end. The pocket cartoonist is imprisoned in a daily sentry box and it was enjoyable to escape the constraints of perennially pushing two characters into an unnatural intimacy and making them pass a convenient newspaper billboard.

Apart from major landmarks like the sinking of Arthur Scargill, the Westland affair and the use of an English base to bomb Libya, the years covered were enlivened by the emergence of Captain Robert Maxwell MC as a national figure, the clawing his way to the deputy chairmanship of the Tory party by Jeffrey Archer, the Johnson Matthey revelations, the Austrians putting anti-freeze in their white wine, Prince Andrew's engagement to 'Fergie' and Rupert Murdoch creating Fortress Wapping.

This collection sees the virtual demise of the Stringalongs. They make one nostalgic appearance here. I cannot entirely explain their eclipse except in terms of the re-emergence of class stereotypes in national life: hog-whimpering young things with their Hooray Henriettas, fat cat lawyers, hanging judges and a new breed of pushy wives. In comparison the home life of a Hampstead pseudo-intellectual became largely irrelevant. But I miss them. Though the cartoonist professionally relishes cads and cock-ups, what remains of him as a human being must wish for a more humane society. But would there be many jokes?

M.B.

‘Excuse me sir, but you’ve inadvertently tucked your shirt tail in’

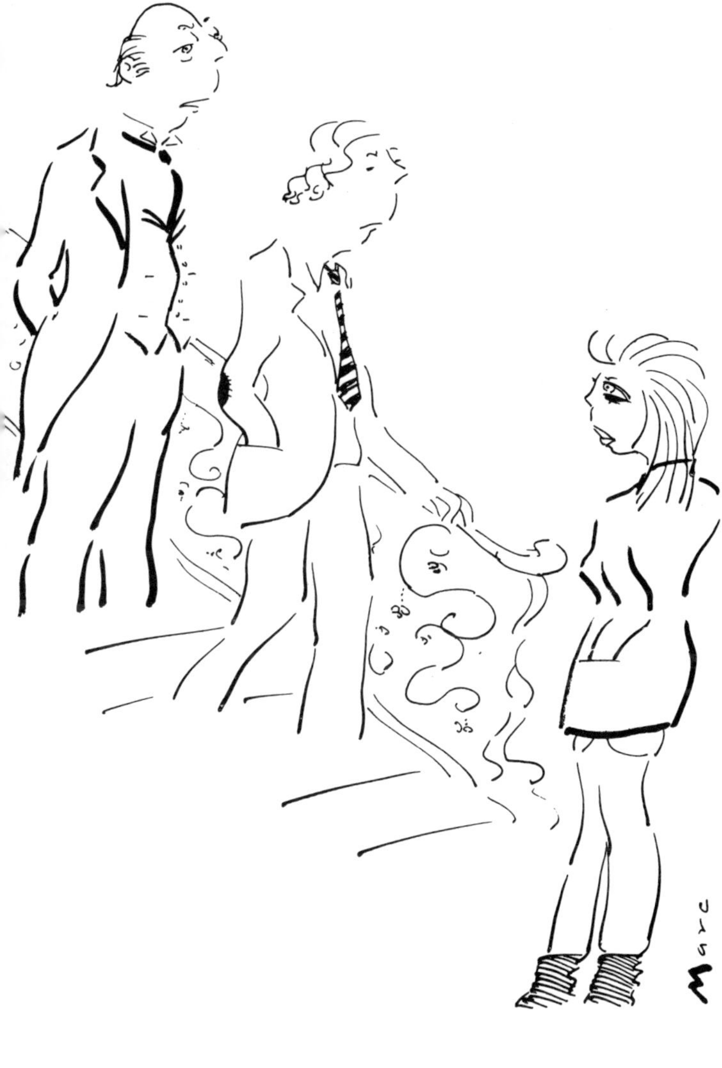

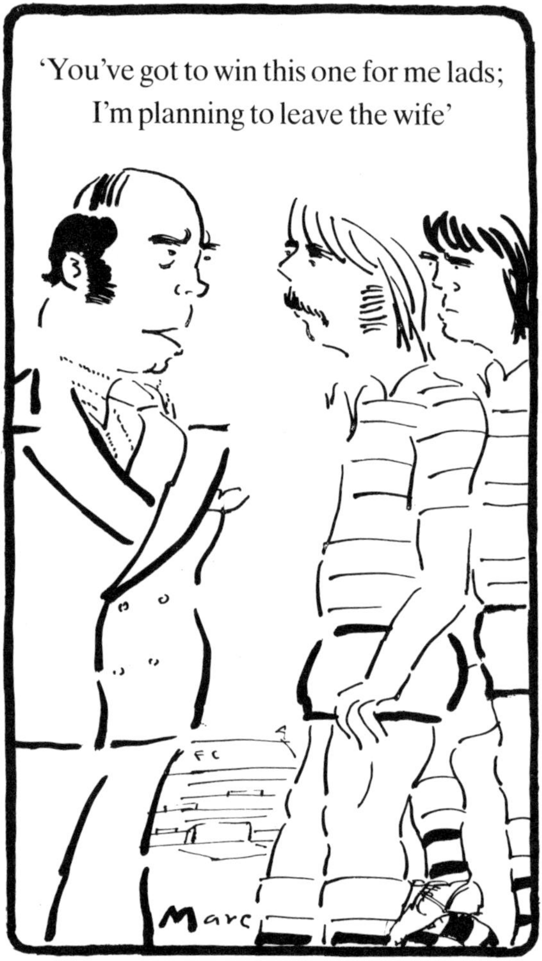

'You've got to win this one for me lads; I'm planning to leave the wife'

The Guardian June 12th 1984

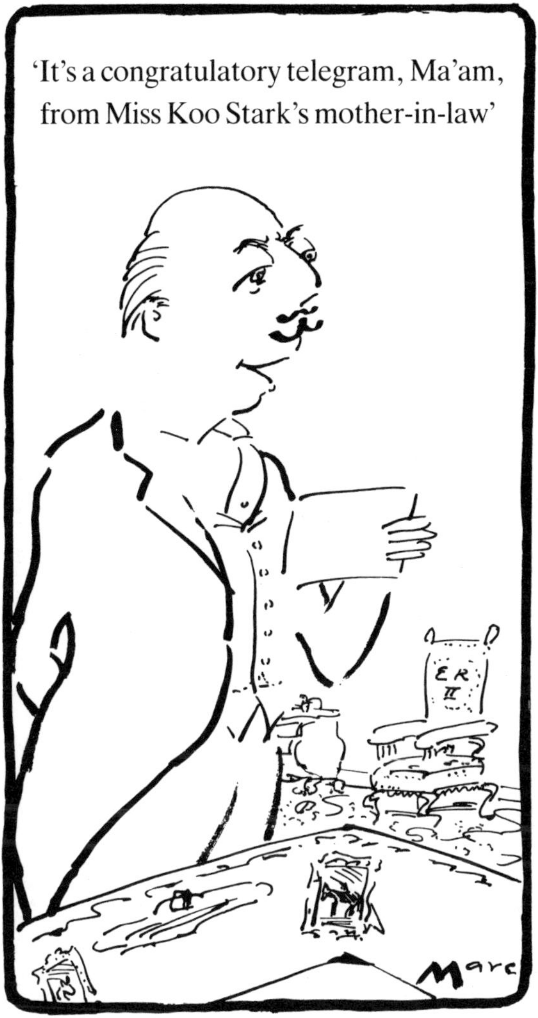

Koo weds
The Guardian August 17th 1984

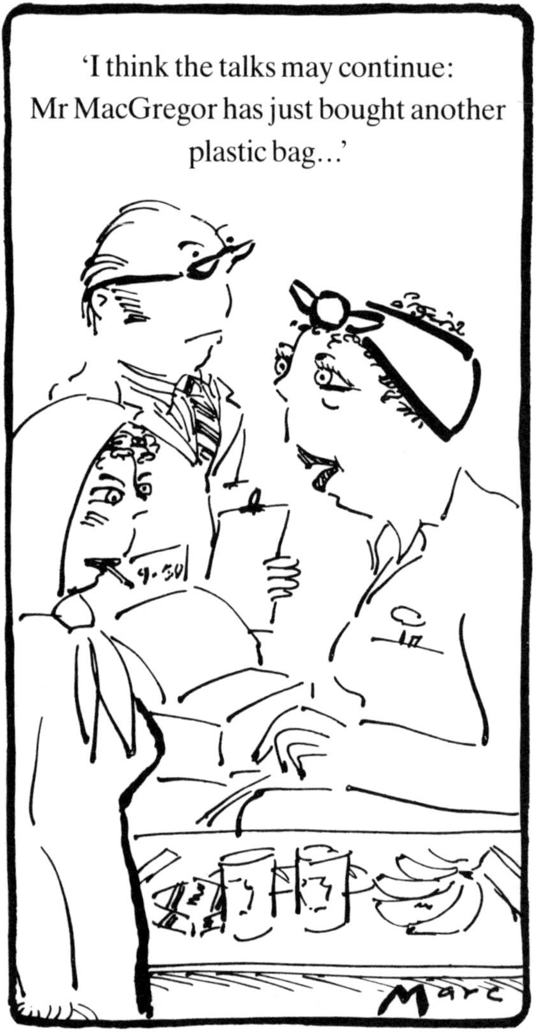

'I think the talks may continue: Mr MacGregor has just bought another plastic bag…'

The miners' strike …
The Guardian September 11th 1984

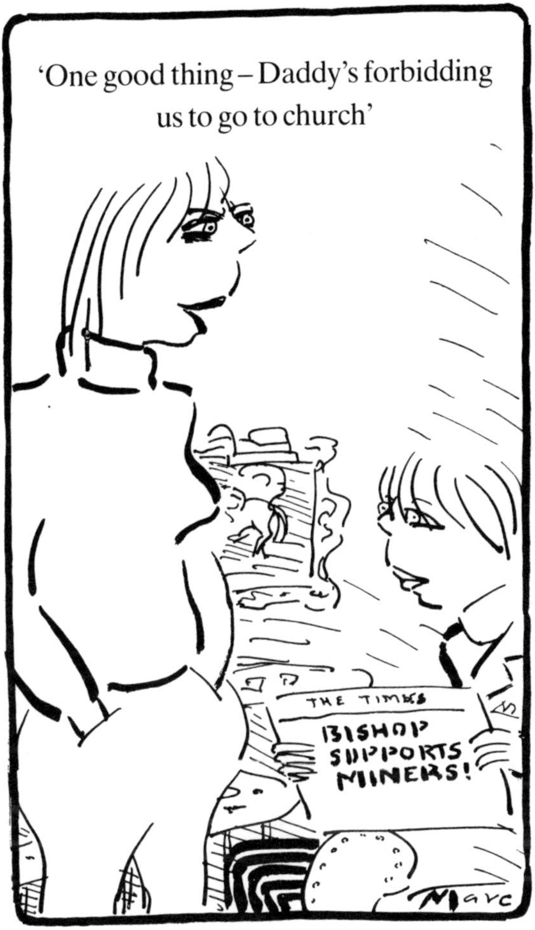

'One good thing – Daddy's forbidding us to go to church'

The Guardian September 25th 1984

'The good news is we've won £40,000; the bad news is the staff have won £100,000'

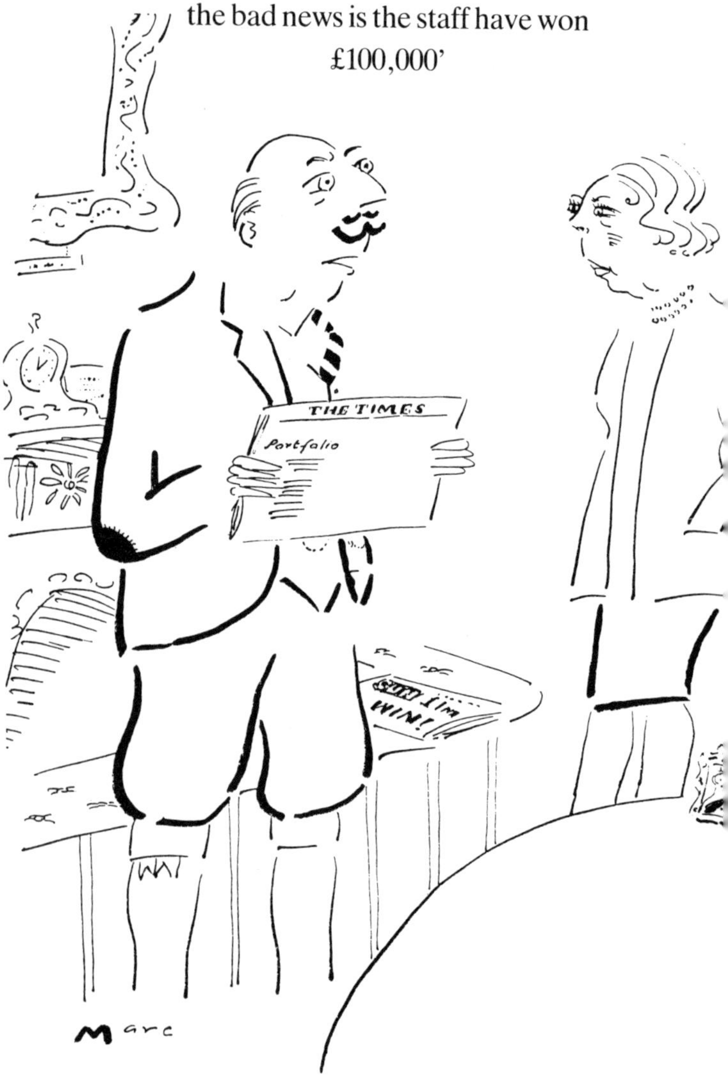

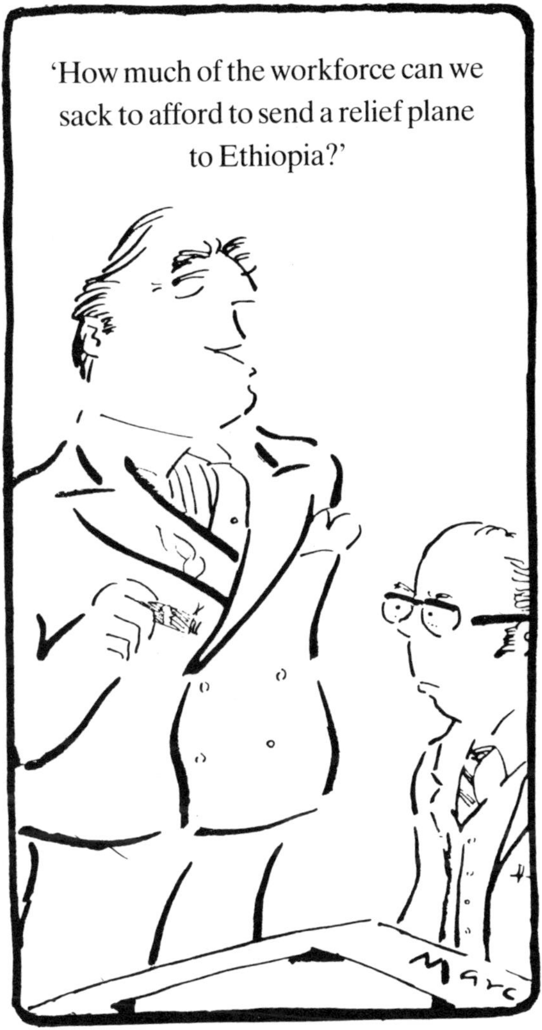

'How much of the workforce can we sack to afford to send a relief plane to Ethiopia?'

The Guardian October 31st 1984

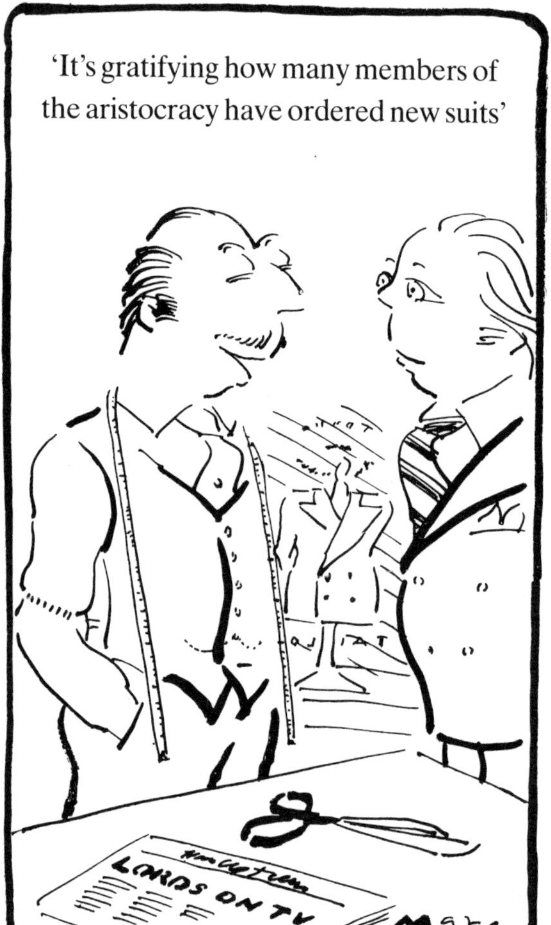

'It's gratifying how many members of the aristocracy have ordered new suits'

The Guardian November 29th 1984

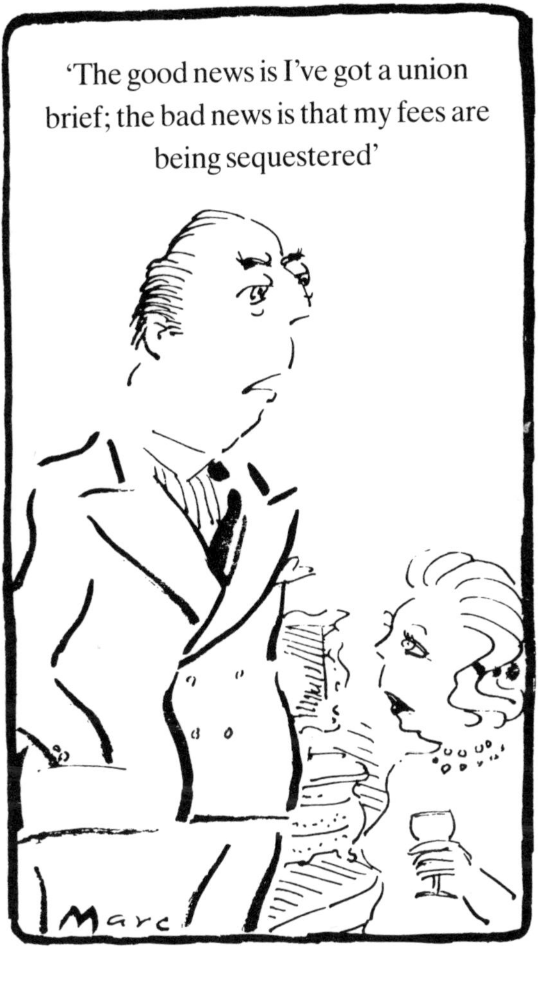

The Guardian December 5th 1984

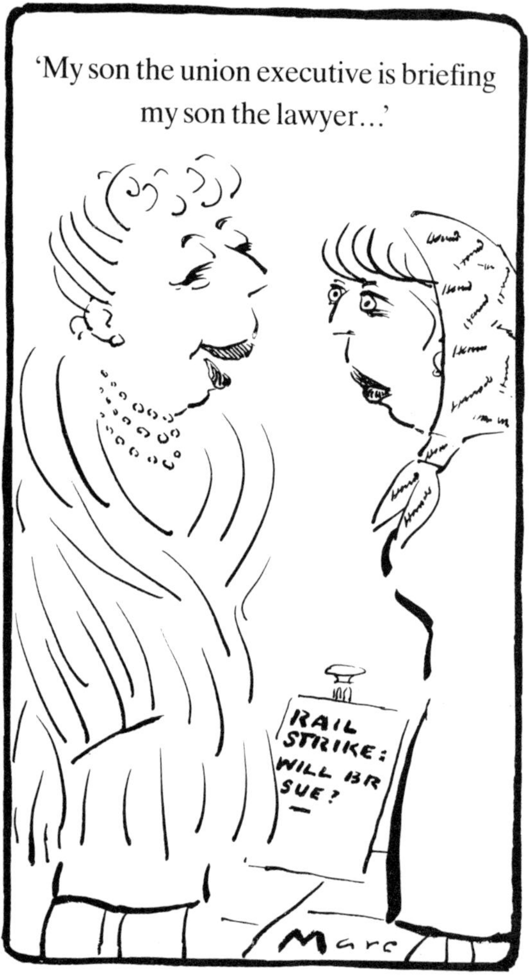

‘My son the union executive is briefing my son the lawyer...’

The Guardian January 18th 1985

'I had this tremendous luck at Heathrow. Customs did me over, but the baggage handlers had already nicked my cocaine'

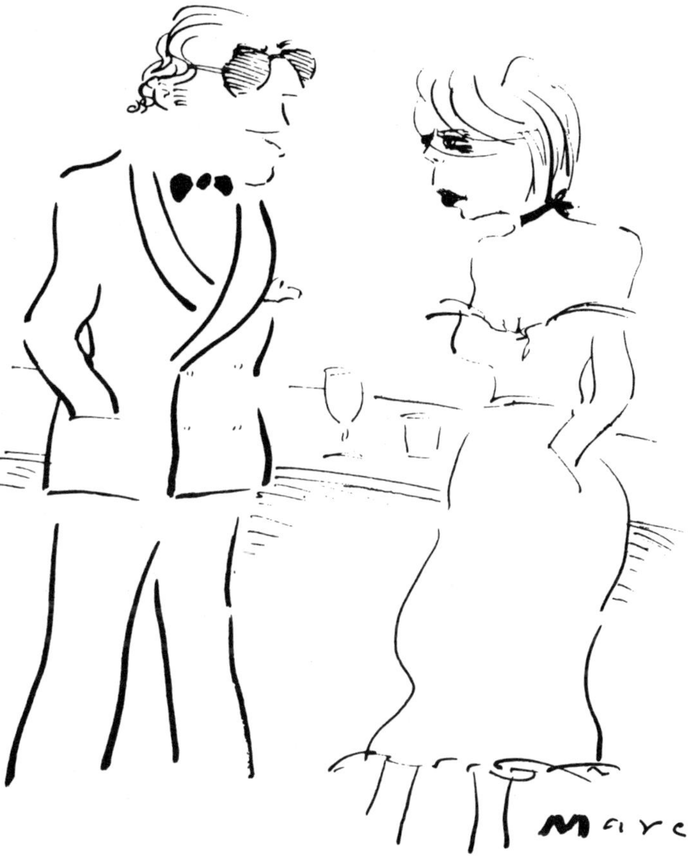

Taki arrested at London airport for importing drugs
June 1984

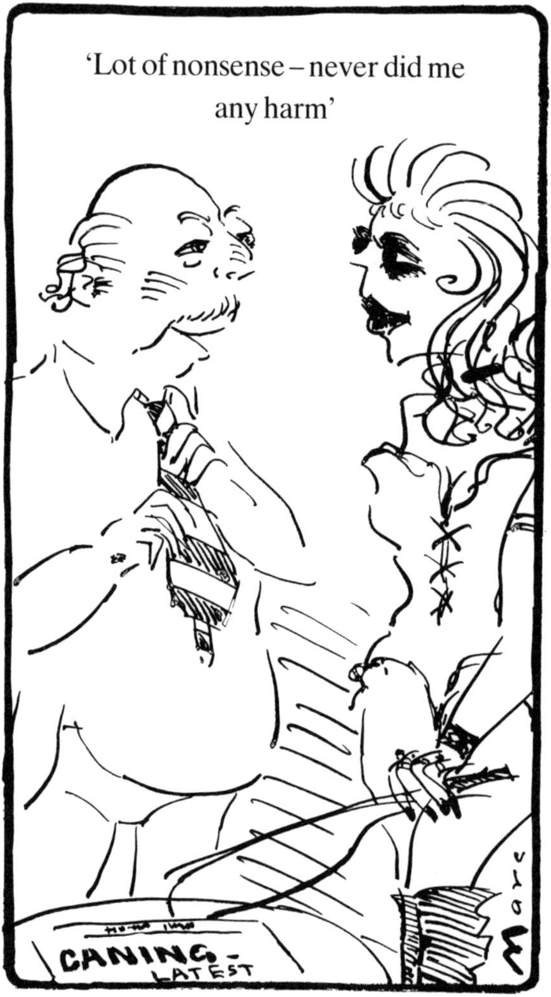

'Lot of nonsense – never did me any harm'

The Guardian January 30th 1985

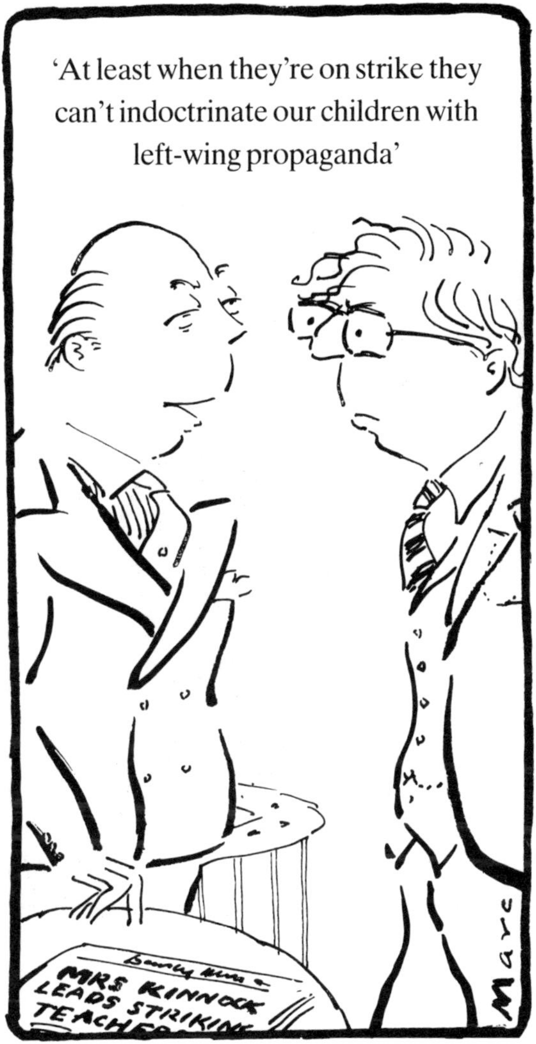

'At least when they're on strike they can't indoctrinate our children with left-wing propaganda'

The Guardian February 28th 1985

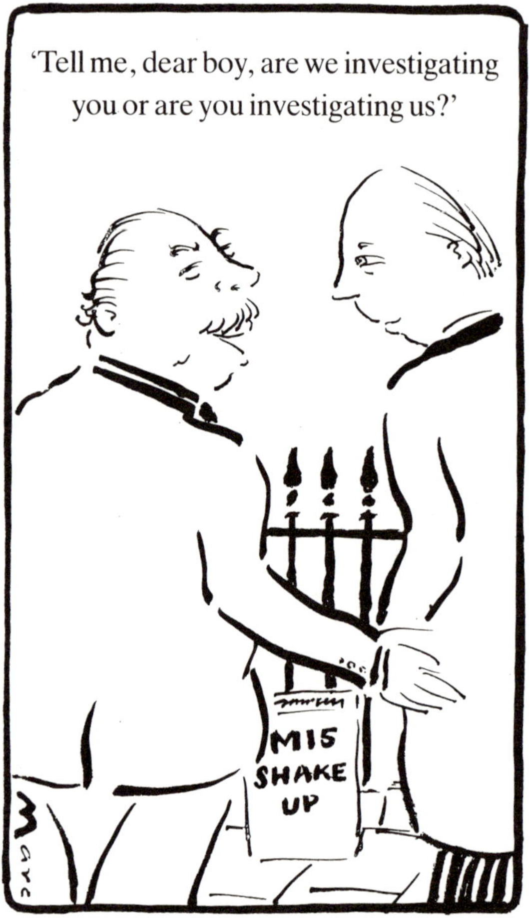

The Guardian March 13th 1985

‘Chelsea: 85 arrests; Newcastle: 98…’

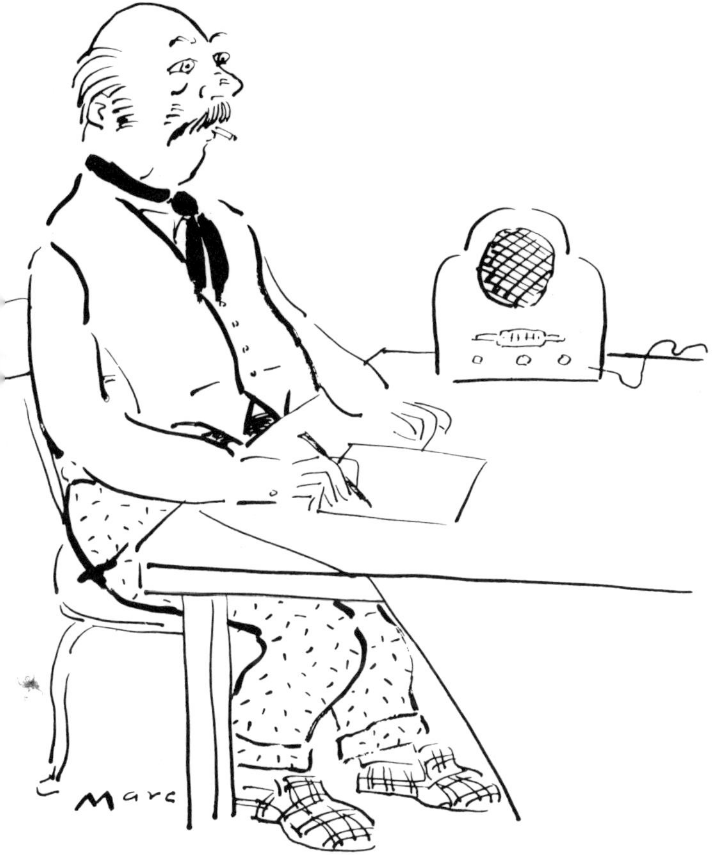

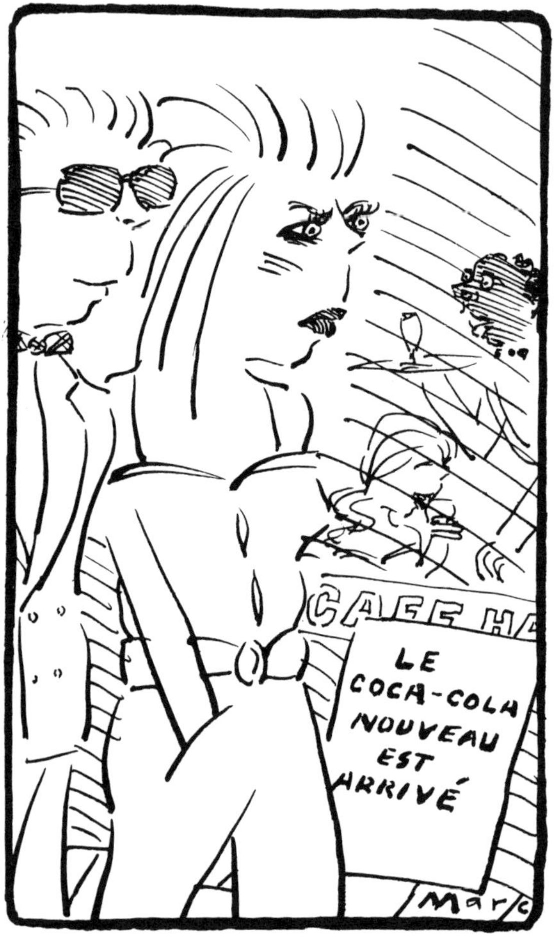

New formula Coca-Cola launched
The Guardian April 26th 1985

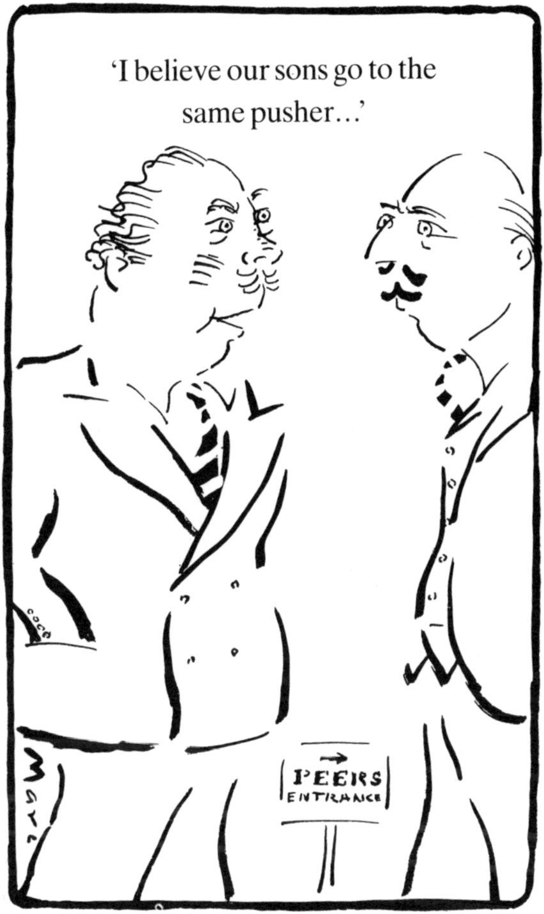

'I believe our sons go to the same pusher…'

The Guardian April 30th 1985

'I'm very worried about Jonathan; he's laughing at the new Kingsley Amis...'

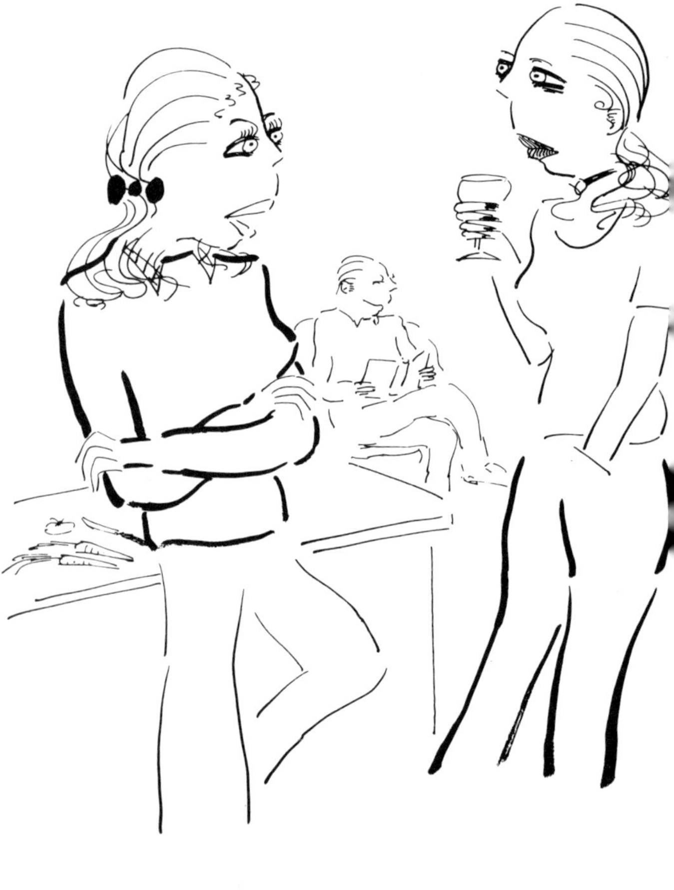

Stanley and the Women published

‘We’re a bit stuck: can you think of a right-wing bishop to marry Fiona?’

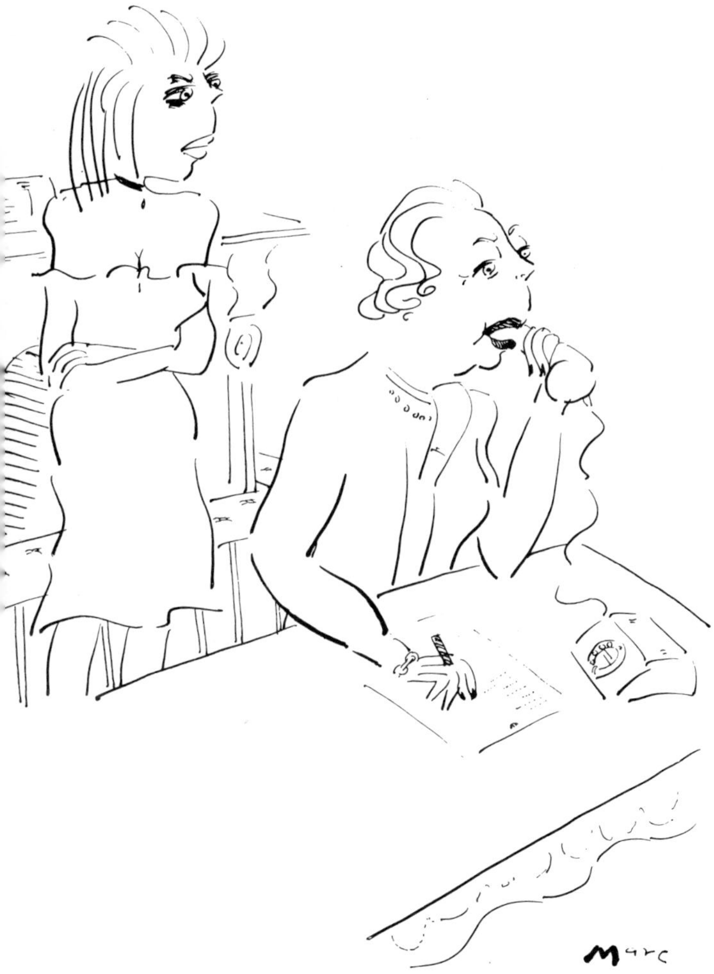

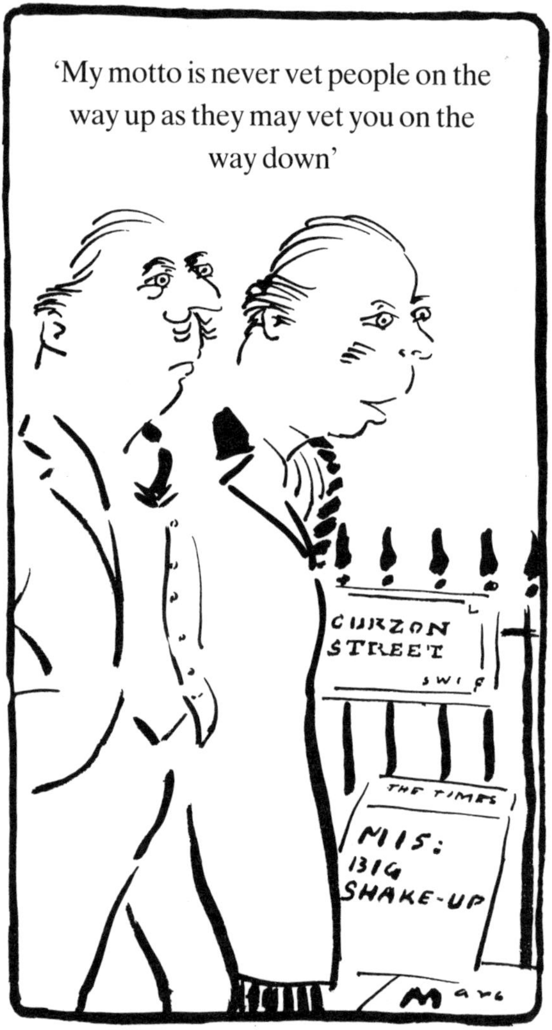

The Guardian May 8th 1985

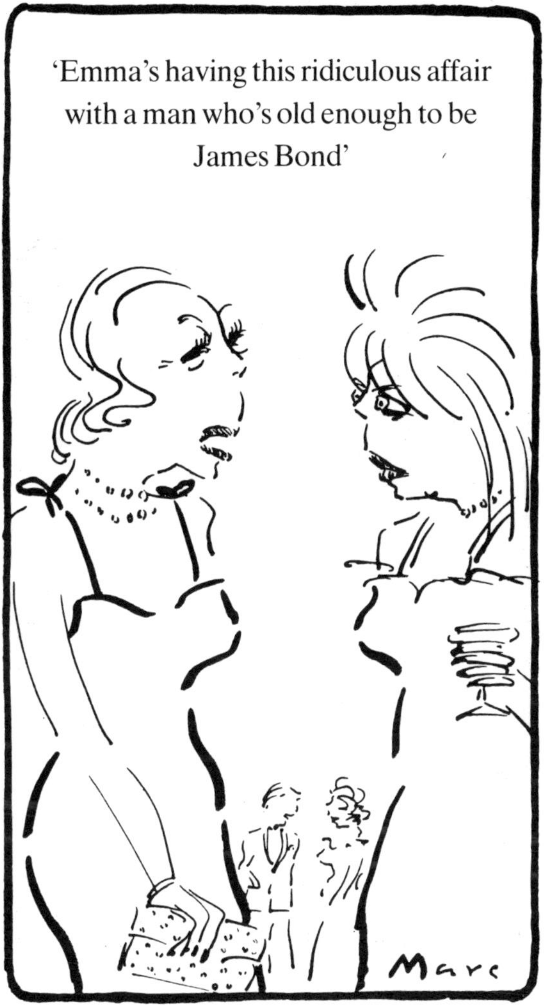

'Emma's having this ridiculous affair with a man who's old enough to be James Bond'

The Guardian June 14th 1985

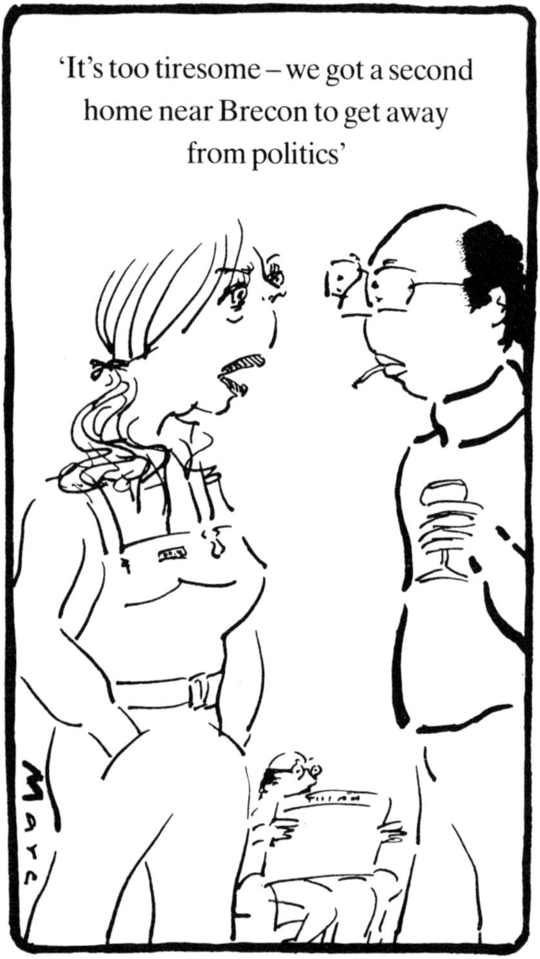

'It's too tiresome – we got a second home near Brecon to get away from politics'

Brecon by-election
The Guardian June 19th 1985

'I'm afraid not. I promised the next piggy-back to Peregrine'

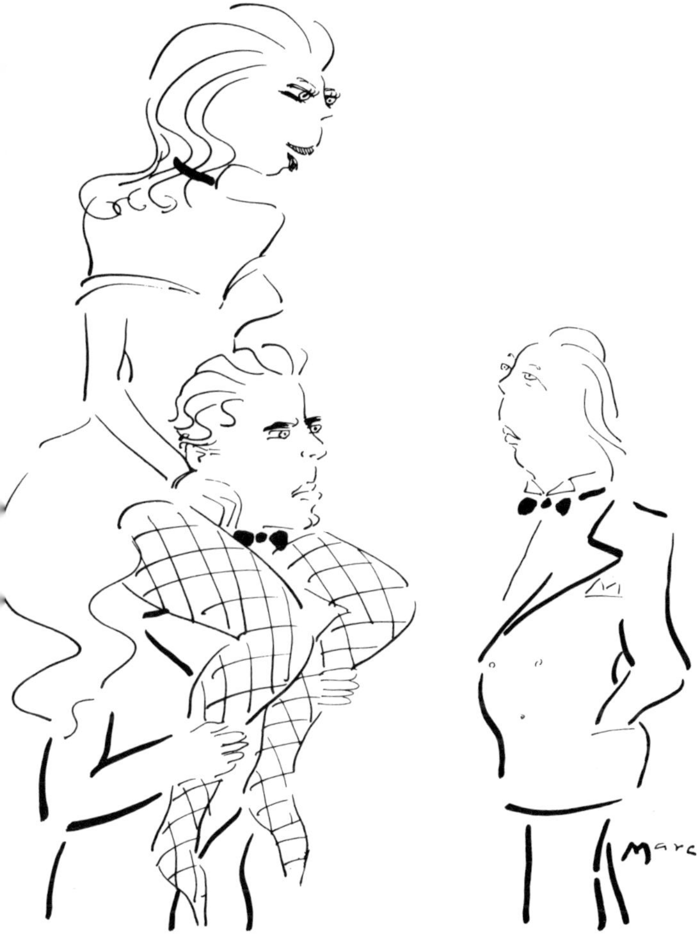

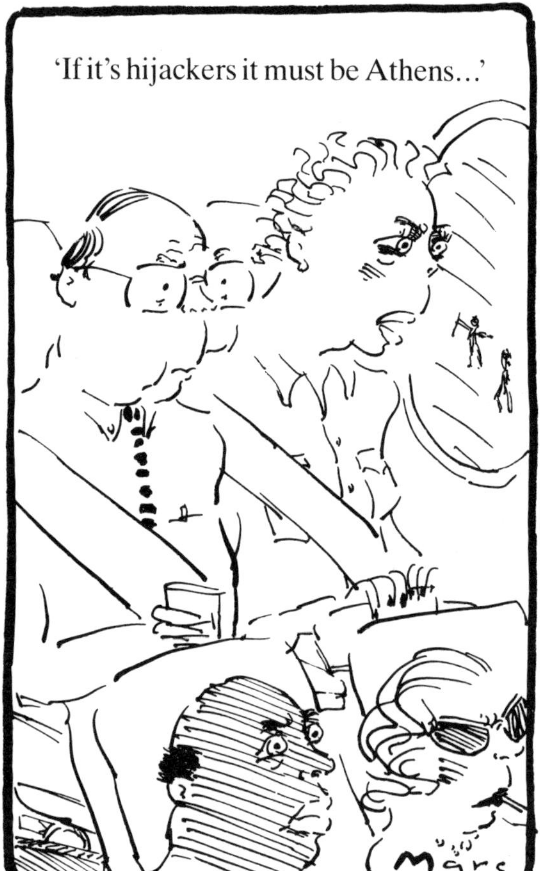

The Guardian June 21st 1985

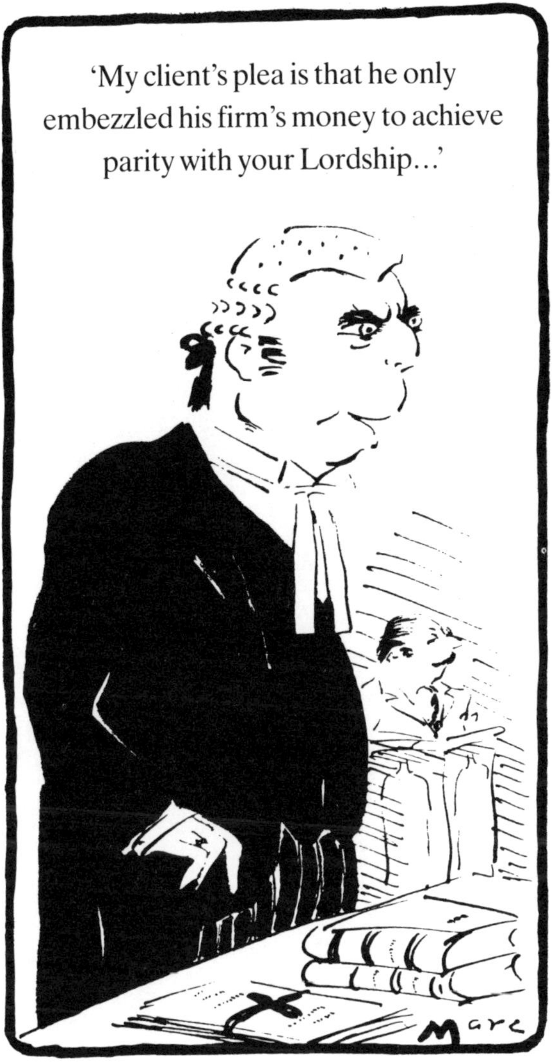

Judges salaries rise dramatically
The Guardian July 23rd 1985

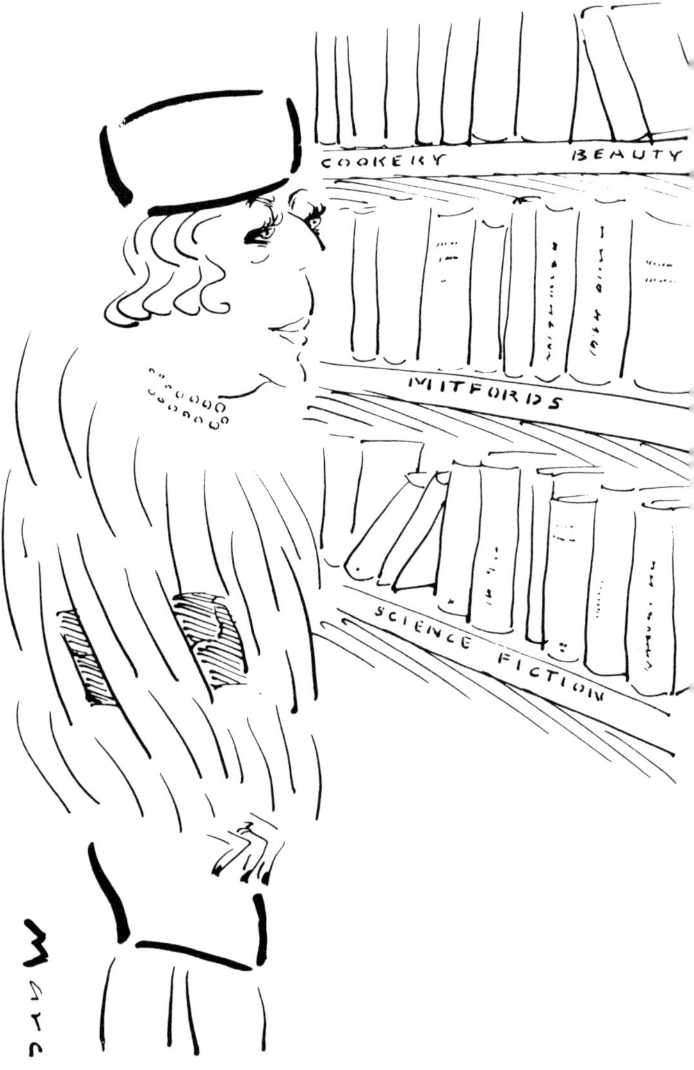

Jonathan and Catherine Guinness's book on the Mitford family published November 1984

'Why don't we try to get a loan from Johnson Matthey to pay our Lawyer's fees?'

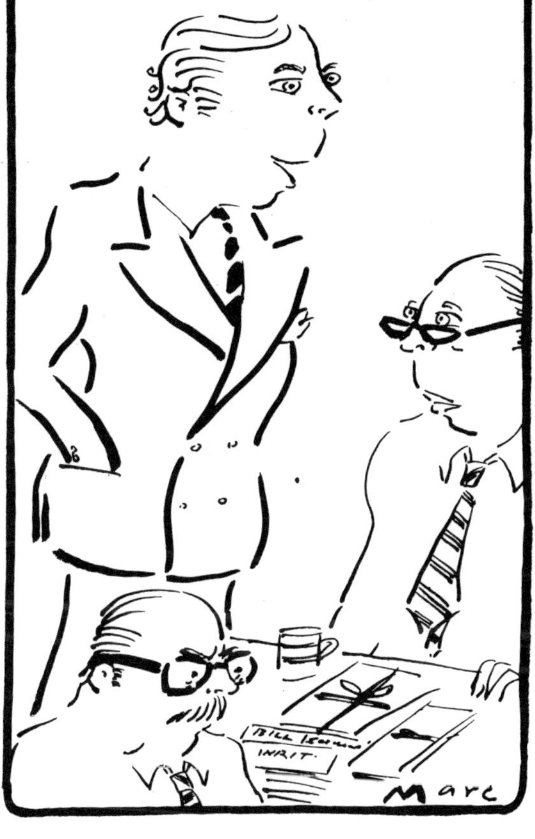

The Guardian July 25th 1985

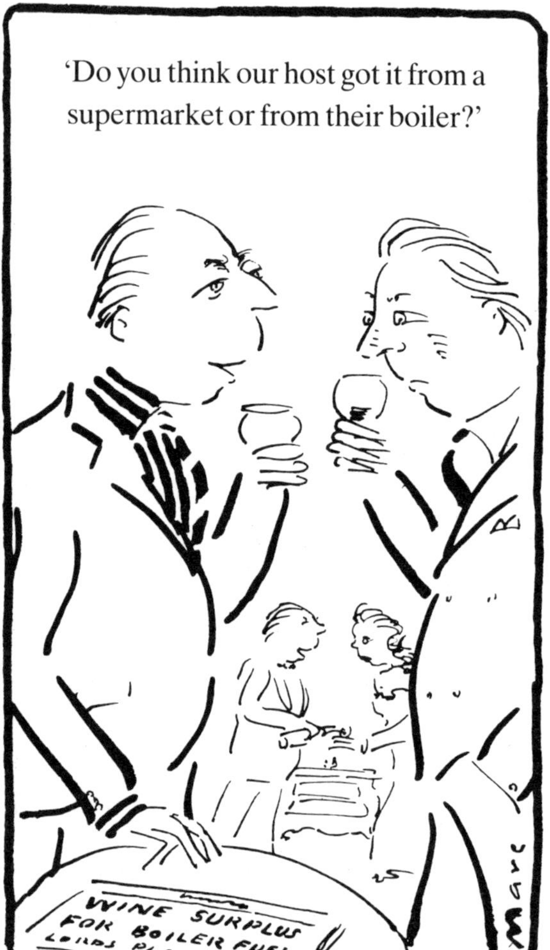

'Do you think our host got it from a supermarket or from their boiler?'

The Guardian July 26th 1985

'I want to make you a star of stage, screen and health and beauty book'

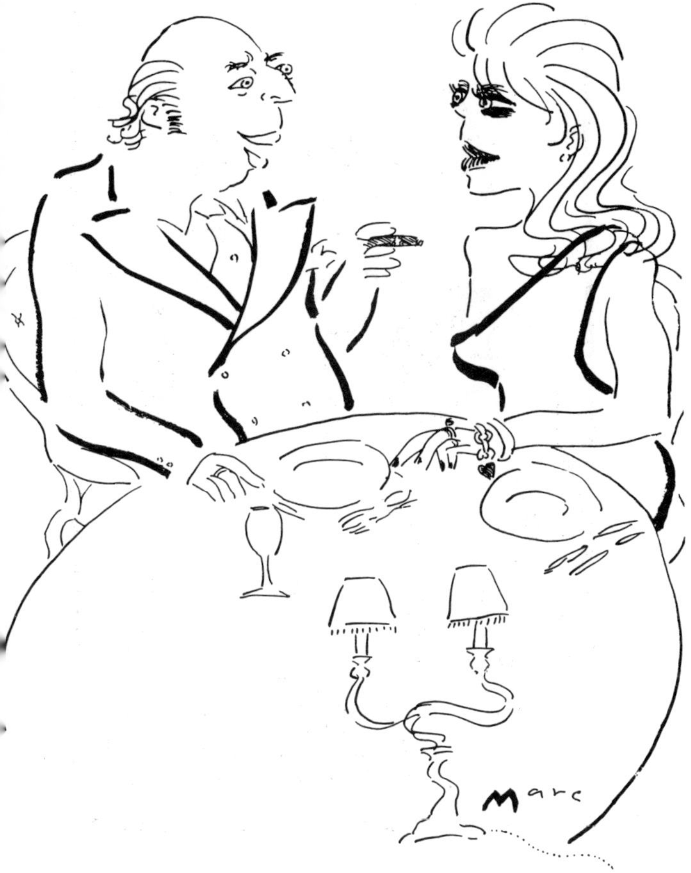

'He's got a problem if the first thing he has to do is find a job for Patrick Jenkin'

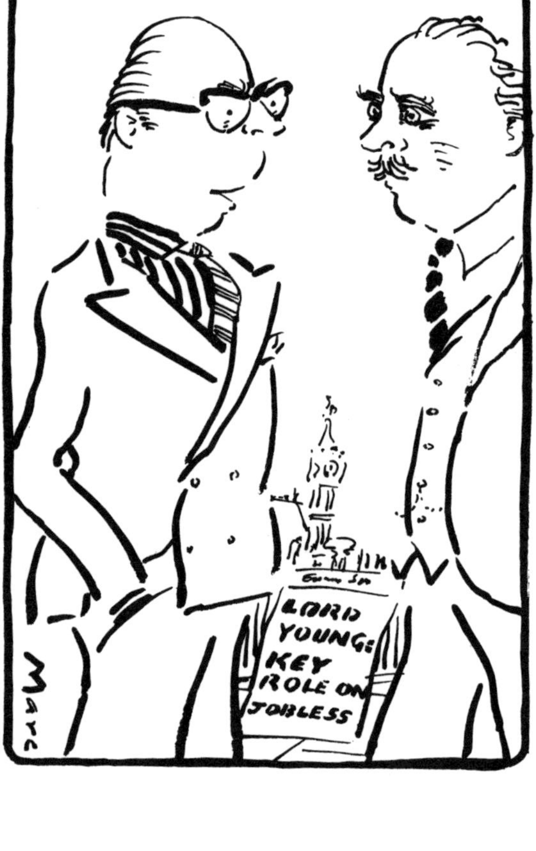

The Guardian September 4th 1985

'He may have won, but *my* sponsor is taking over *his* sponsor...'

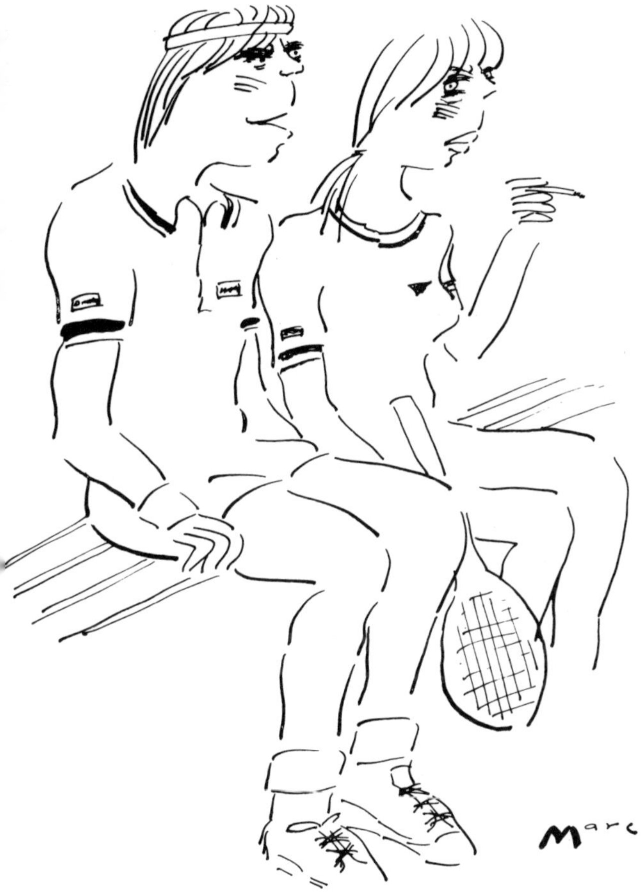

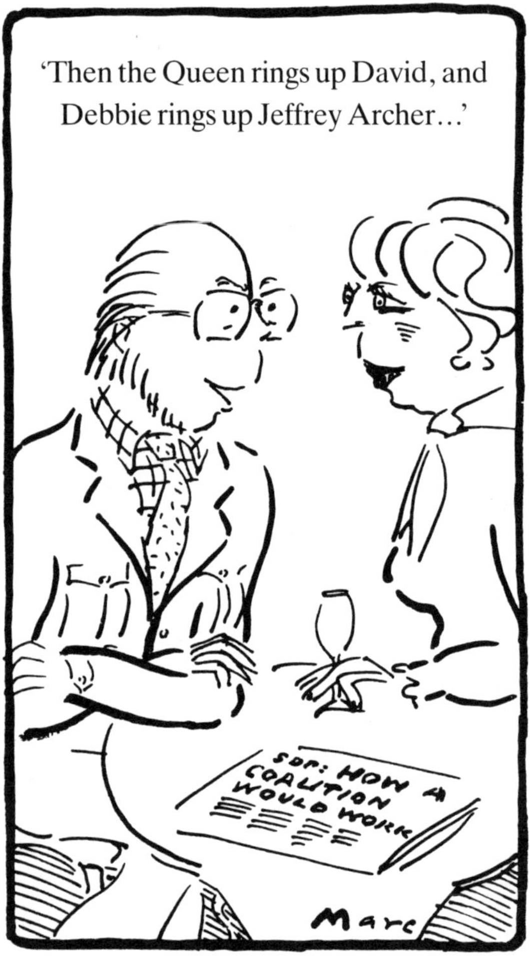

'Then the Queen rings up David, and Debbie rings up Jeffrey Archer...'

Coalition speculation
The Guardian September 13th 1985

'Business is booming. We used to make motorways; now we repair them...'

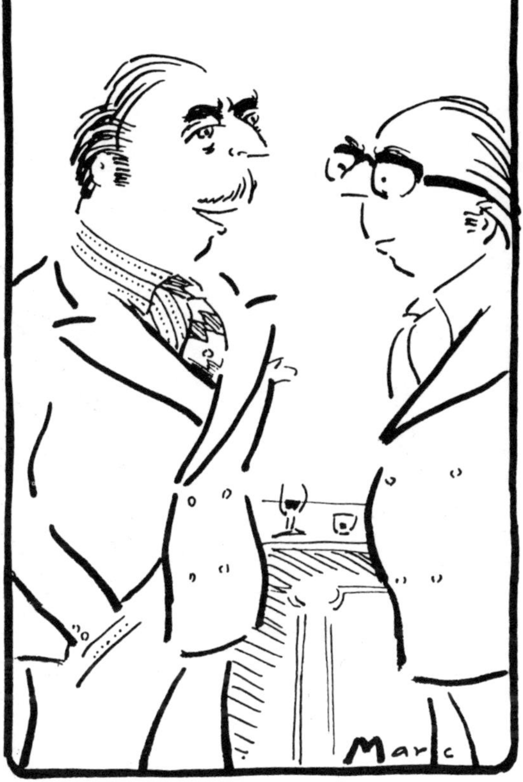

The Guardian September 19th 1985

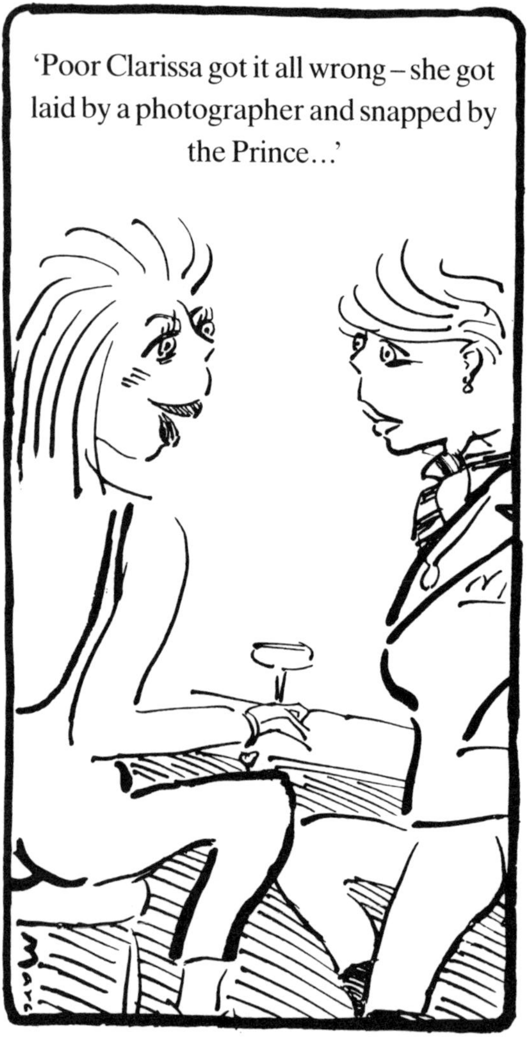

'Poor Clarissa got it all wrong – she got laid by a photographer and snapped by the Prince...'

The Guardian October 3rd 1985

‘His mother was only in animal experiments, but his father is a sniffer dog’

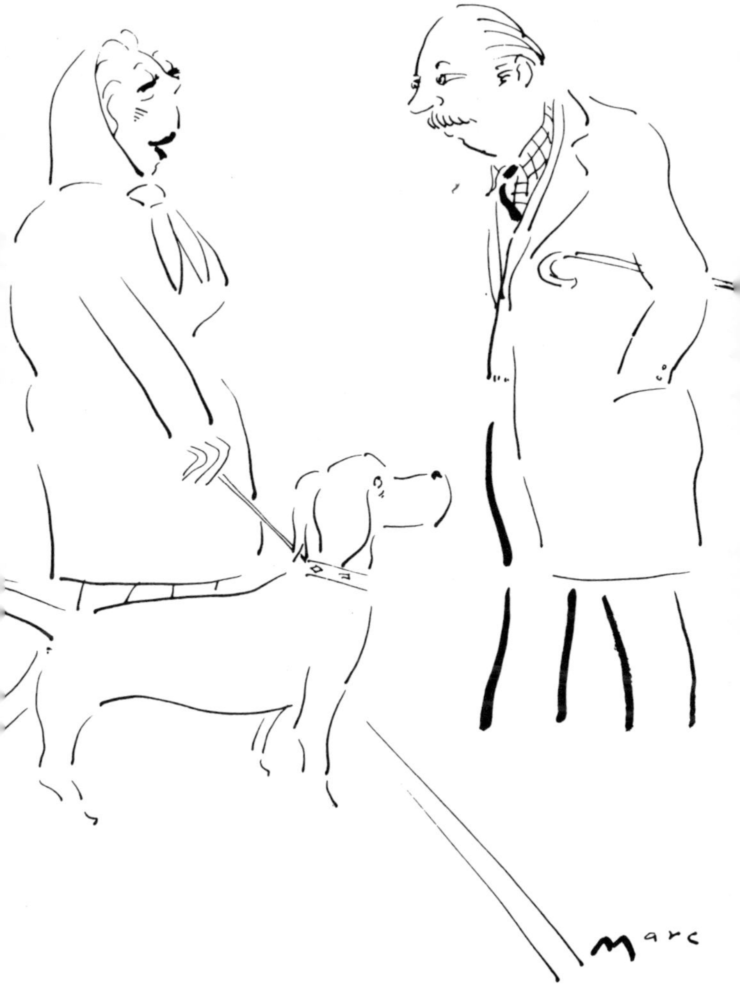

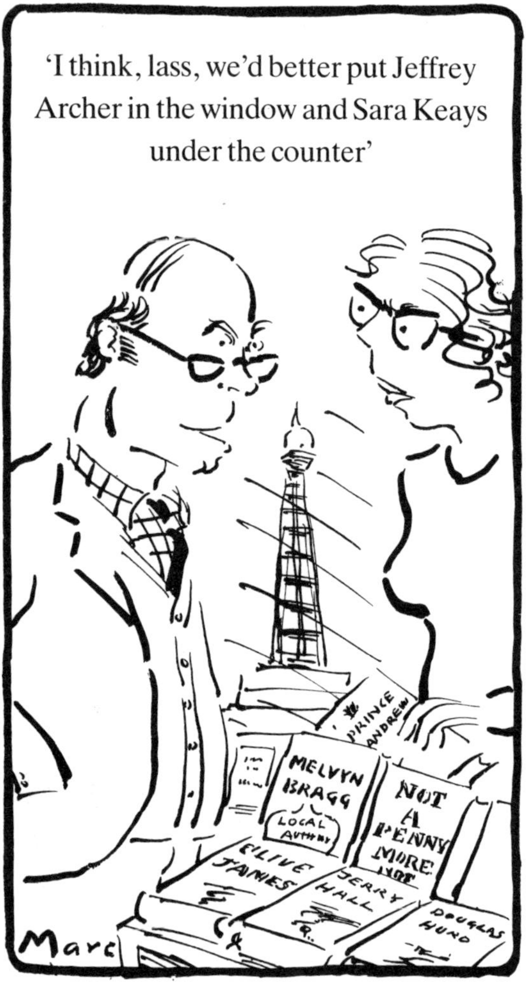

'I think, lass, we'd better put Jeffrey Archer in the window and Sara Keays under the counter'

Tory Party conference
The Guardian October 8th 1985

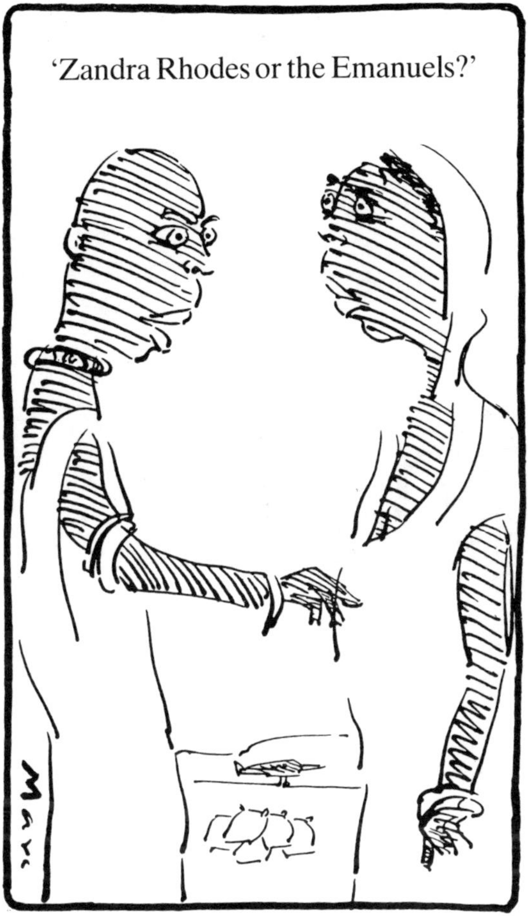

'Zandra Rhodes or the Emanuels?'

Fashion Aid at the Royal Albert Hall
The Guardian November 7th 1985

'Extraordinary – that chappie behind the bar knowing I'm the squire...'

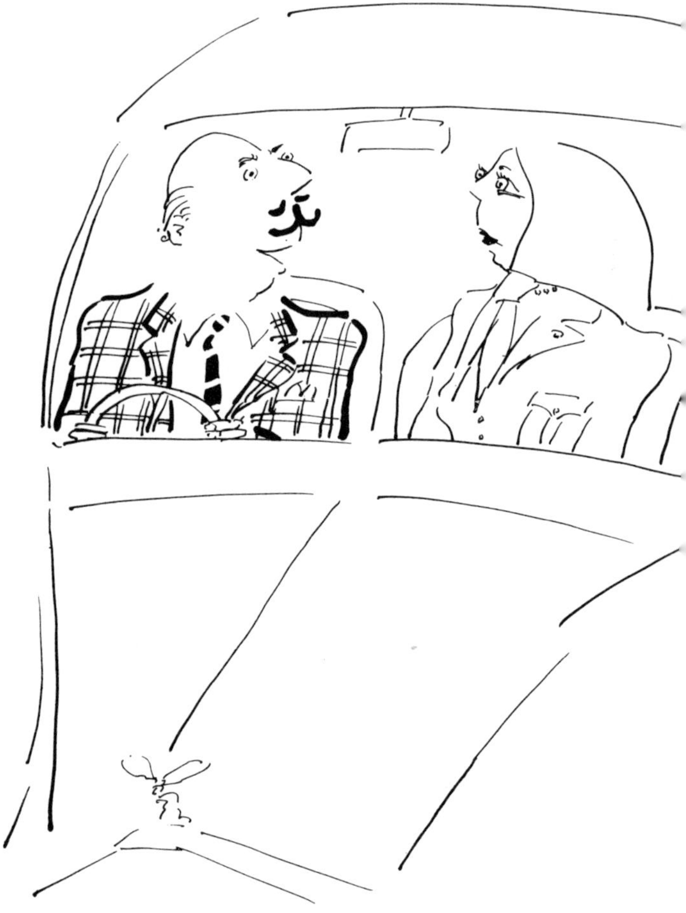

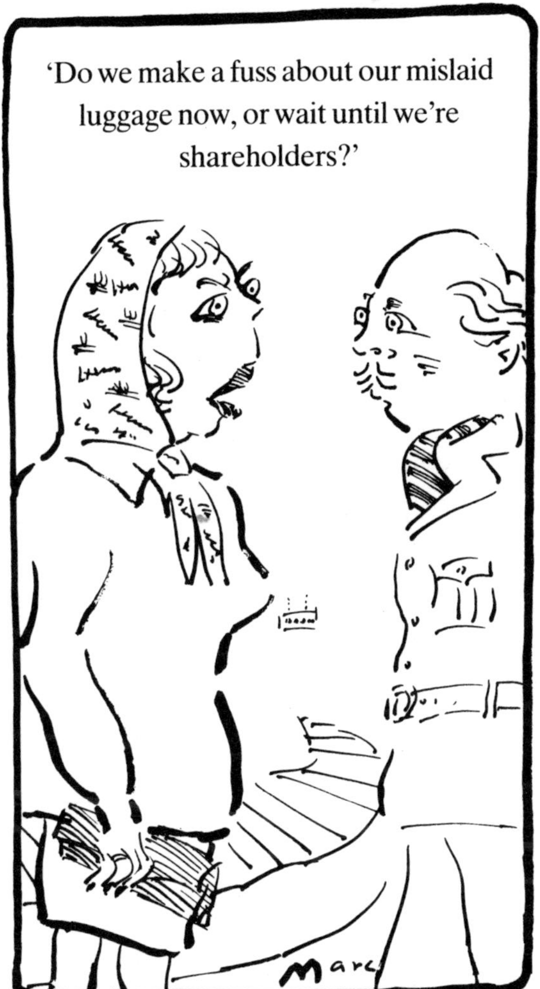

'Do we make a fuss about our mislaid luggage now, or wait until we're shareholders?'

The Guardian November 8th 1985

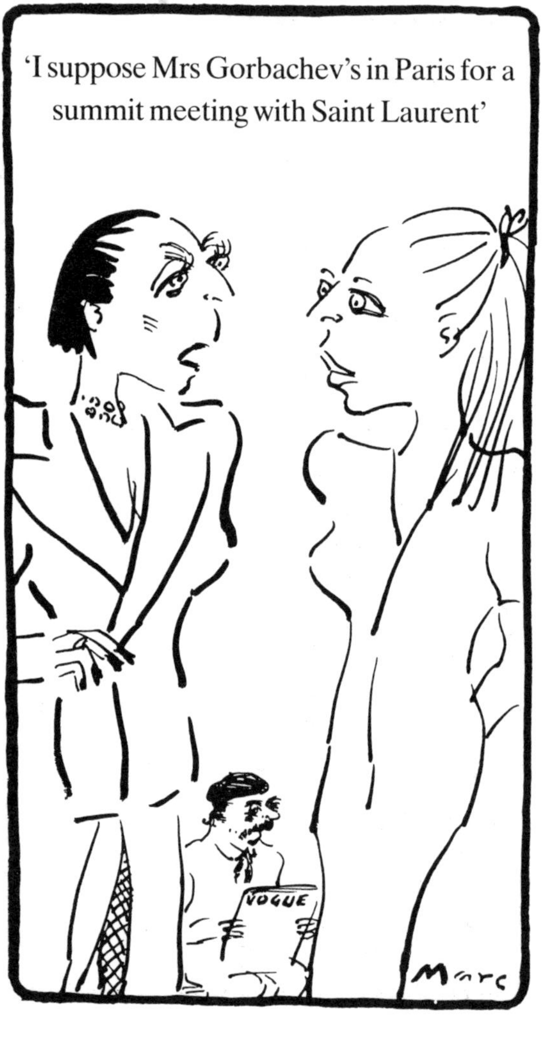

The summit
The Guardian October 4th 1985

'Did you prefer the boys who looked like girls, or the girls who looked like boys?'

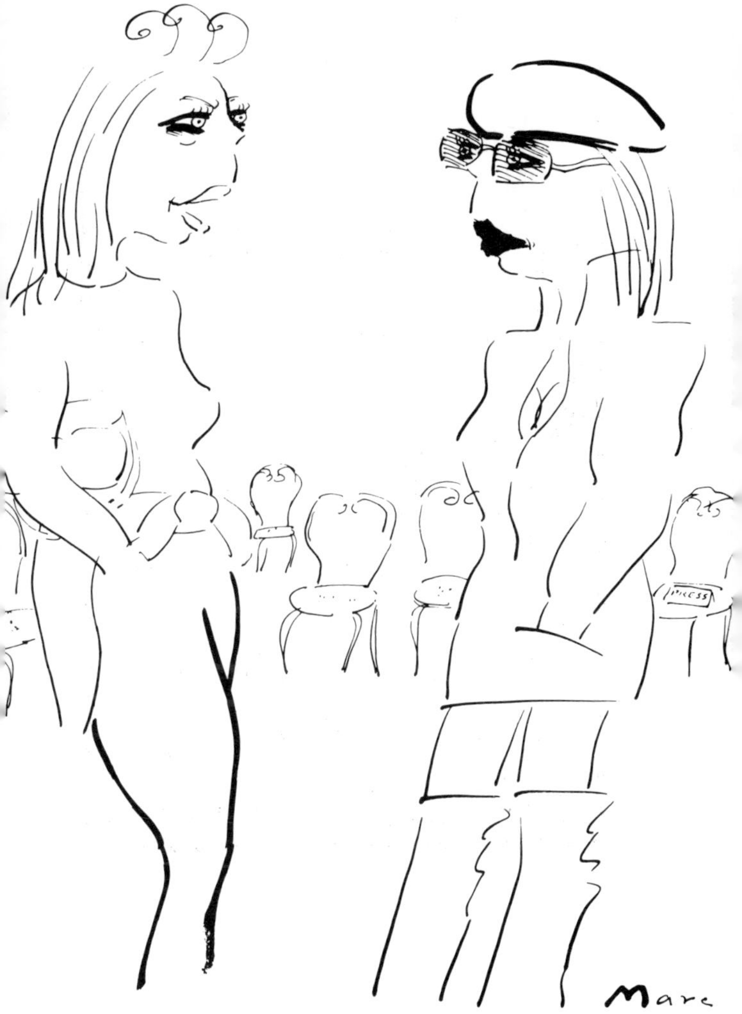

'Gerald can't decide whether he should accept a peerage and be seen asleep on TV, or stay in the House and be shown drunk'

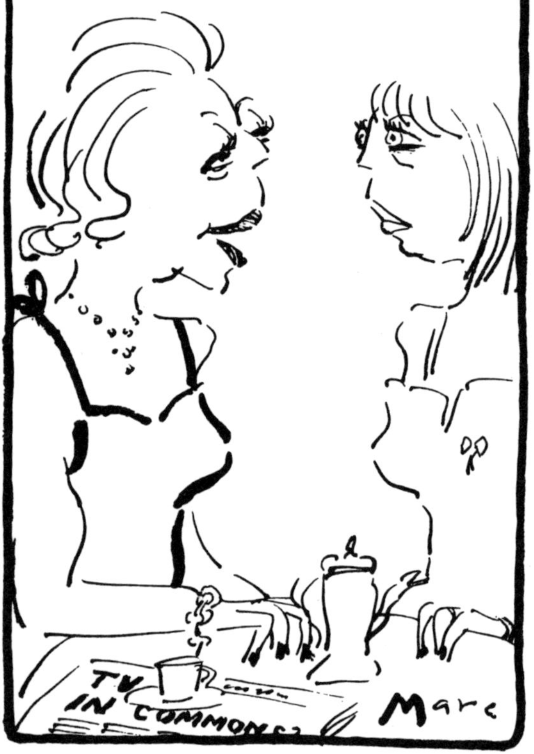

The Guardian November 20th 1985

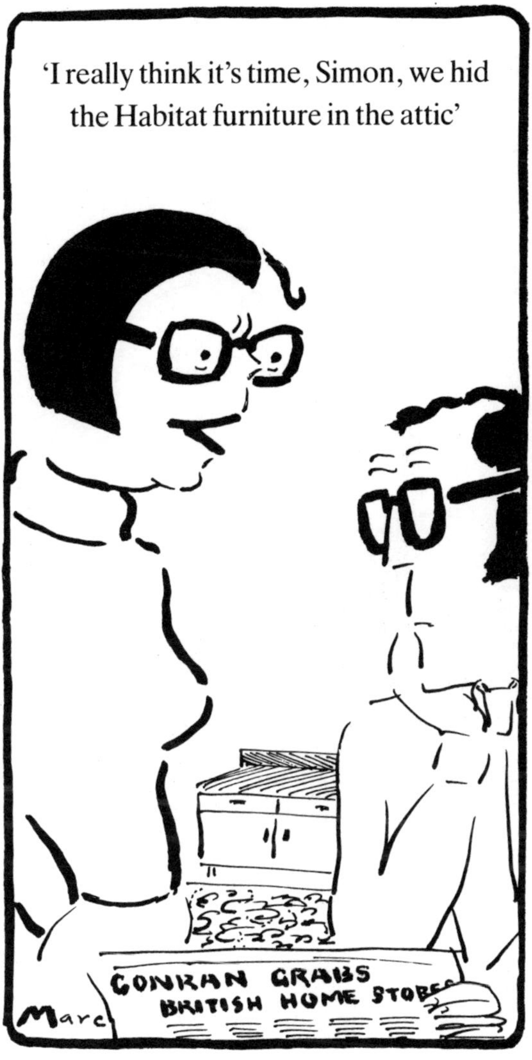

'I really think it's time, Simon, we hid the Habitat furniture in the attic'

The Guardian November 27th 1985

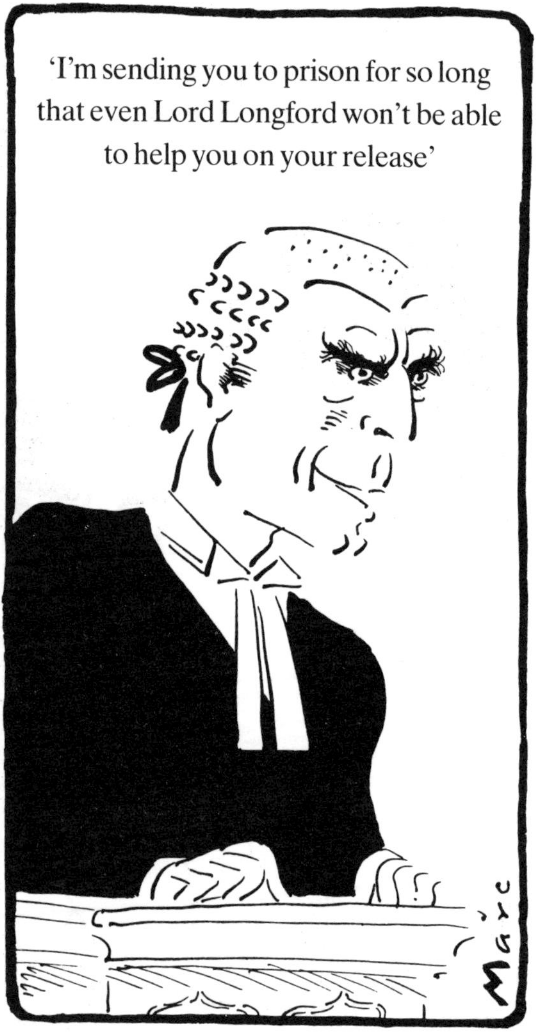

The Guardian November 26th 1985

‘You was on Soccer Special again tonight, Trev...’

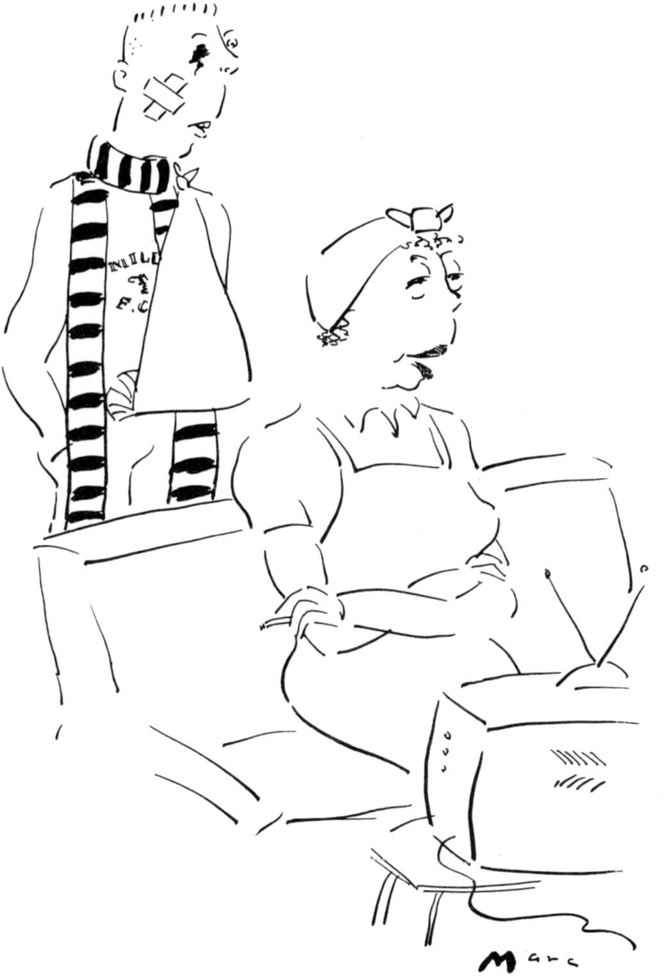

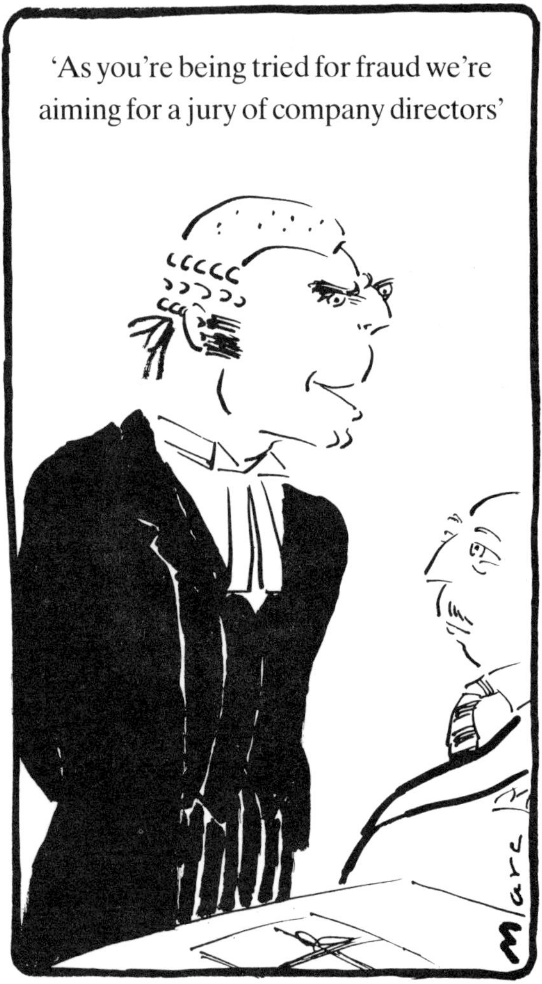

The Guardian November 28th 1985

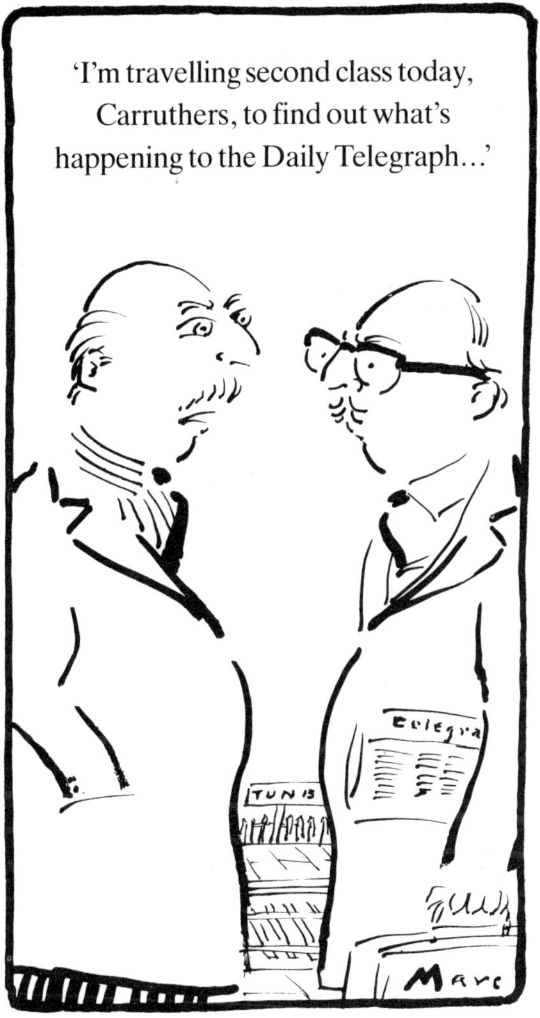

Lord Hartwell forced to sell the Telegraph
to Conrad Black
The Guardian December 11th 1985

'Charles is working late at the bank on a scheme to issue British Airways shares to floating voters...'

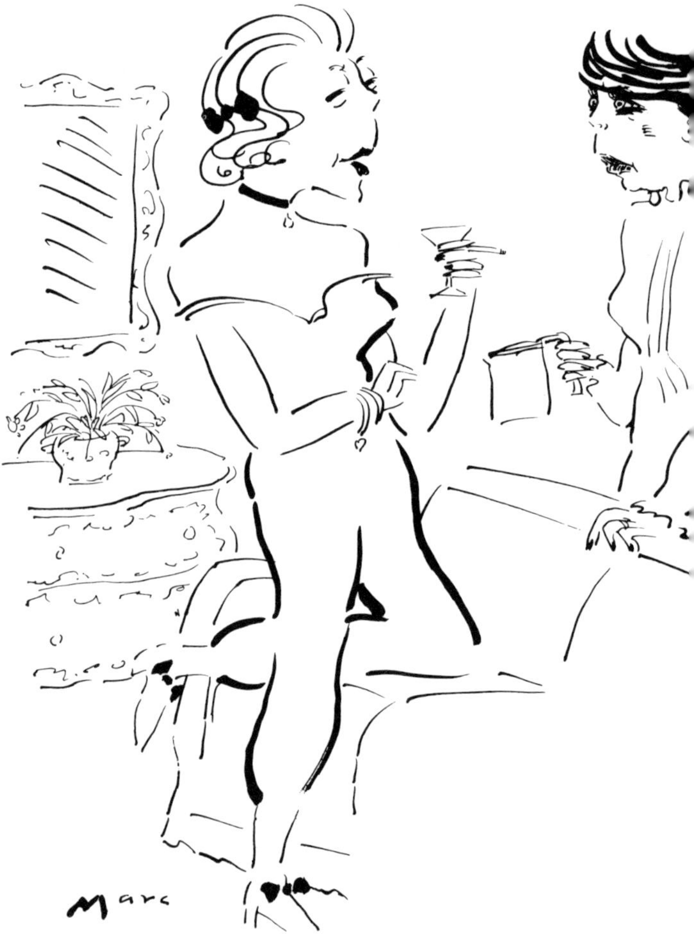

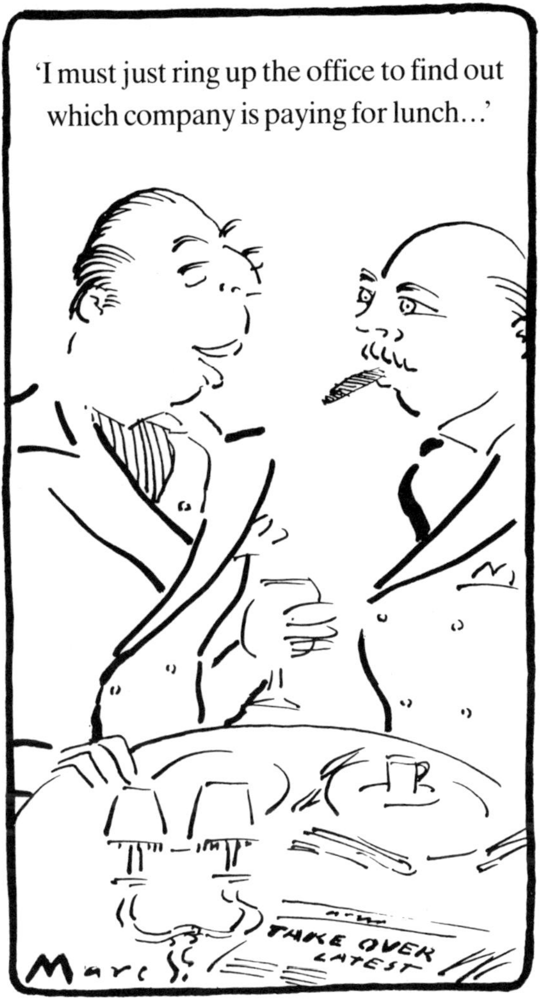

'I must just ring up the office to find out which company is paying for lunch…'

The Guardian December 12th 1985

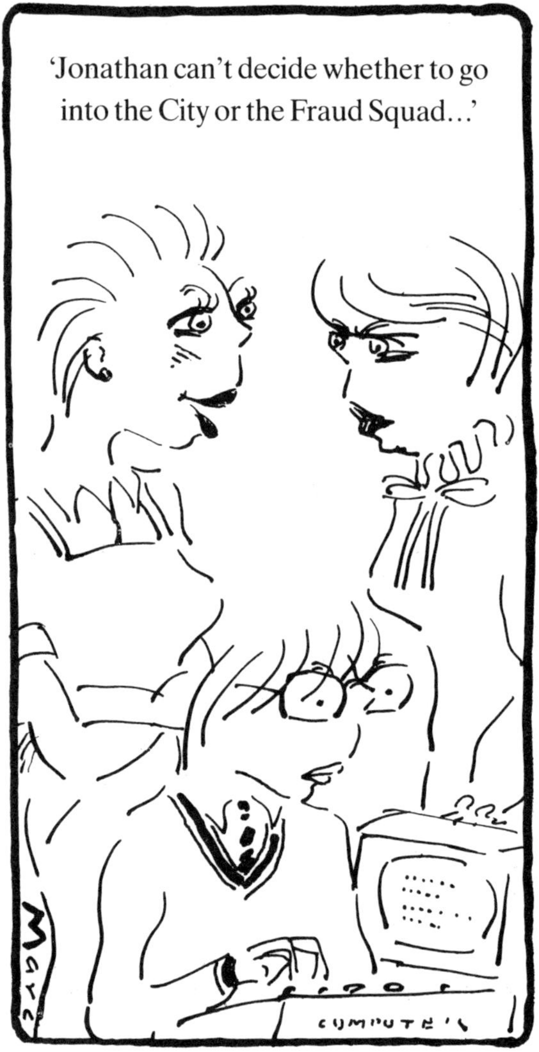

The Guardian December 13th 1985

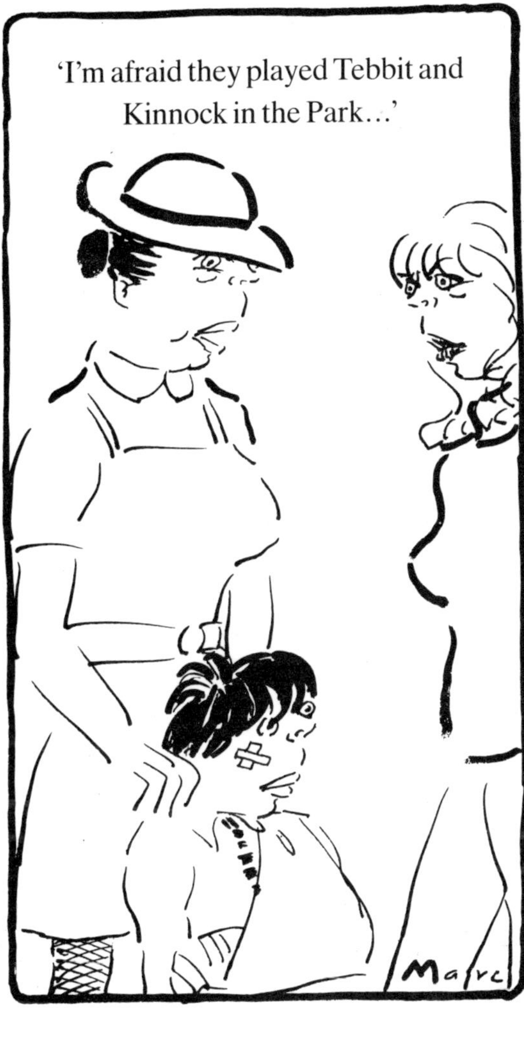

'I'm afraid they played Tebbit and Kinnock in the Park...'

The Guardian December 17th 1985

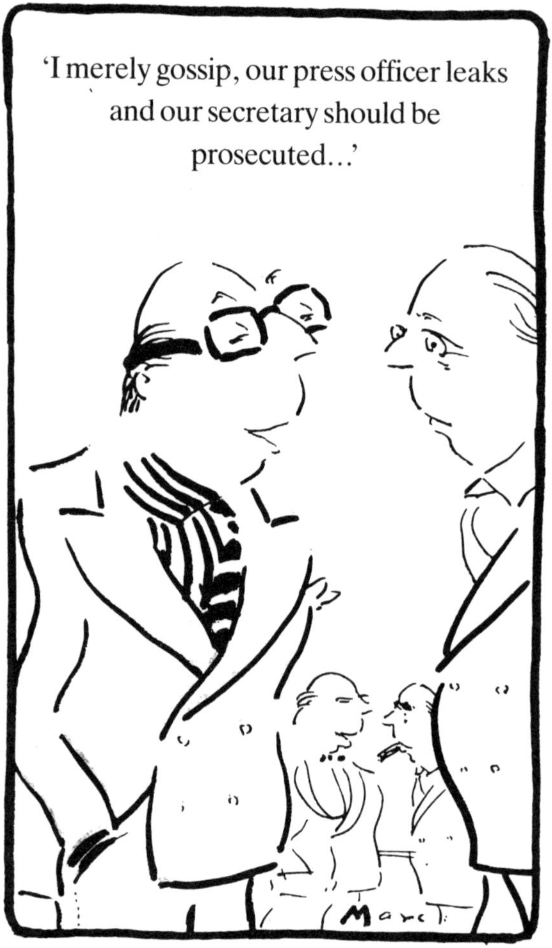

'I merely gossip, our press officer leaks and our secretary should be prosecuted...'

The Westland affair
The Guardian January 23rd 1986

'Imagine the target is a chat show host...'

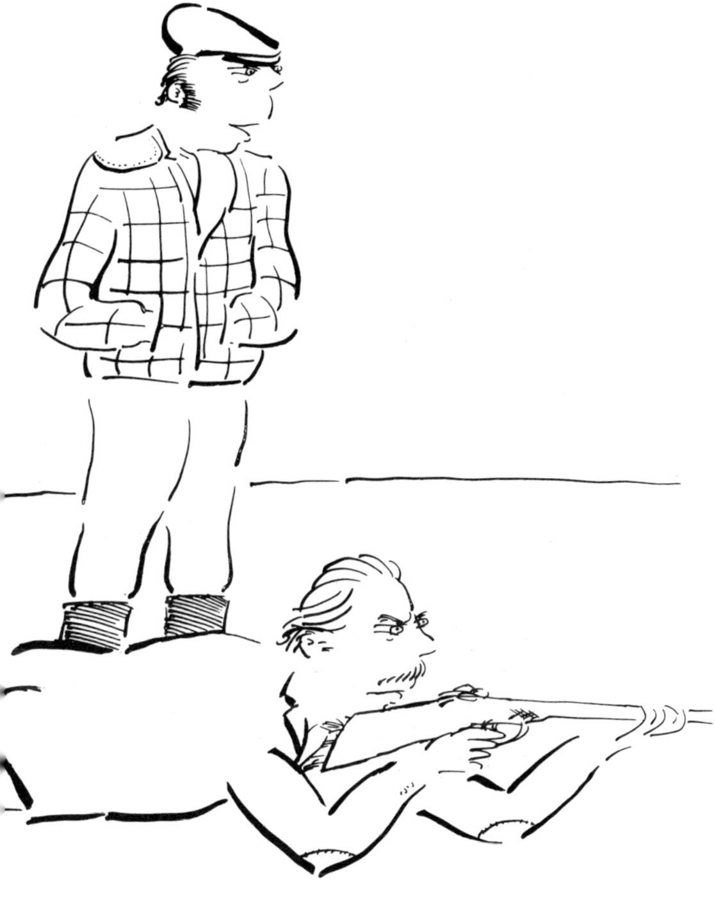

Terry Wogan's show attacked
January 1986

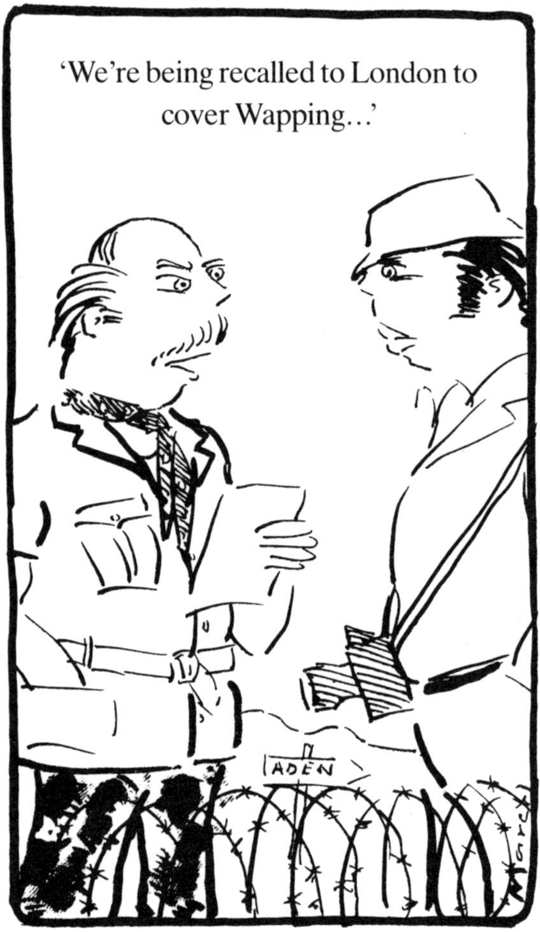

The Guardian January 24th 1986

'No, I didn't know the departed. My car won't start...'

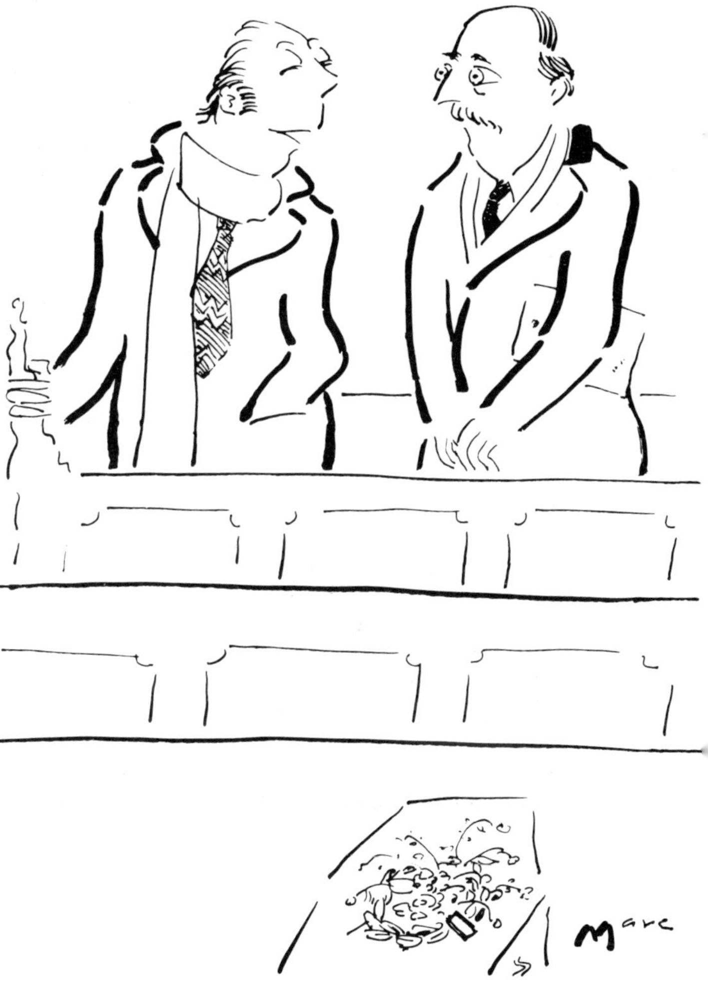

Winter, 1985

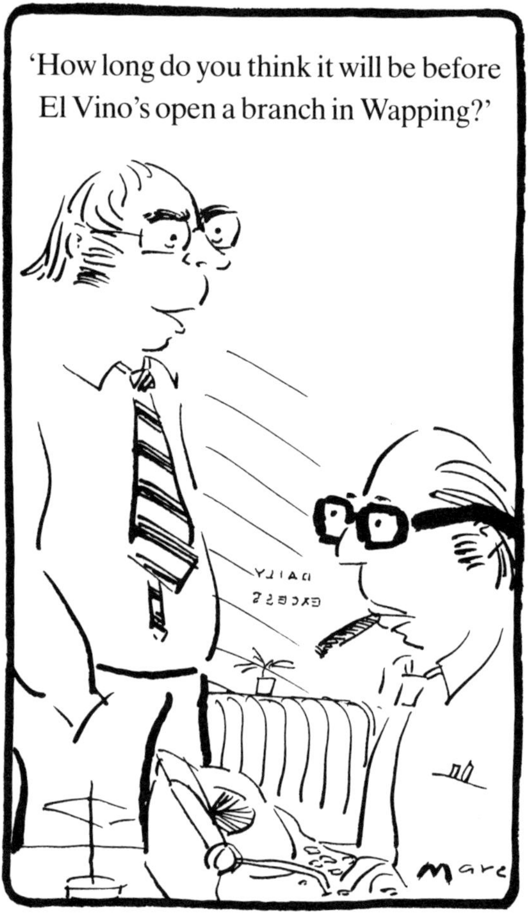

'How long do you think it will be before El Vino's open a branch in Wapping?'

The Guardian January 30th 1986

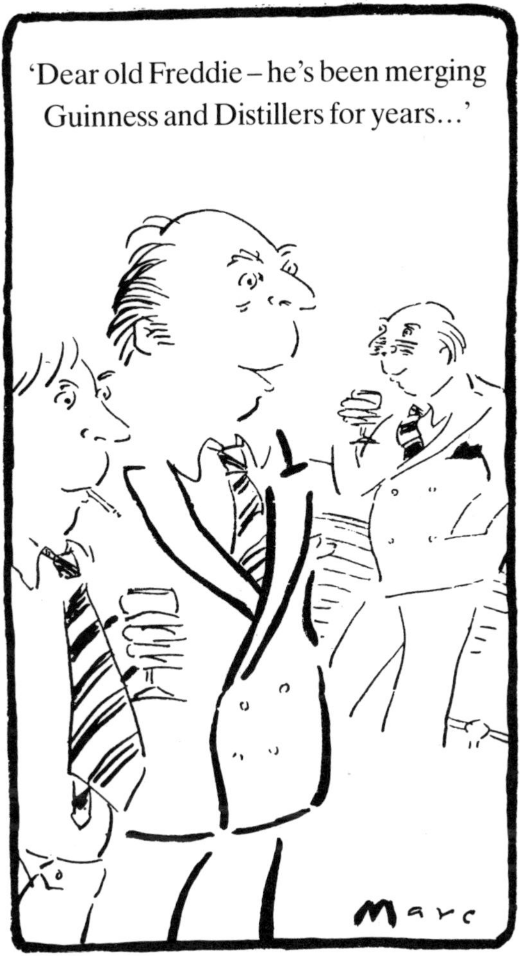

The Guardian February 4th 1986

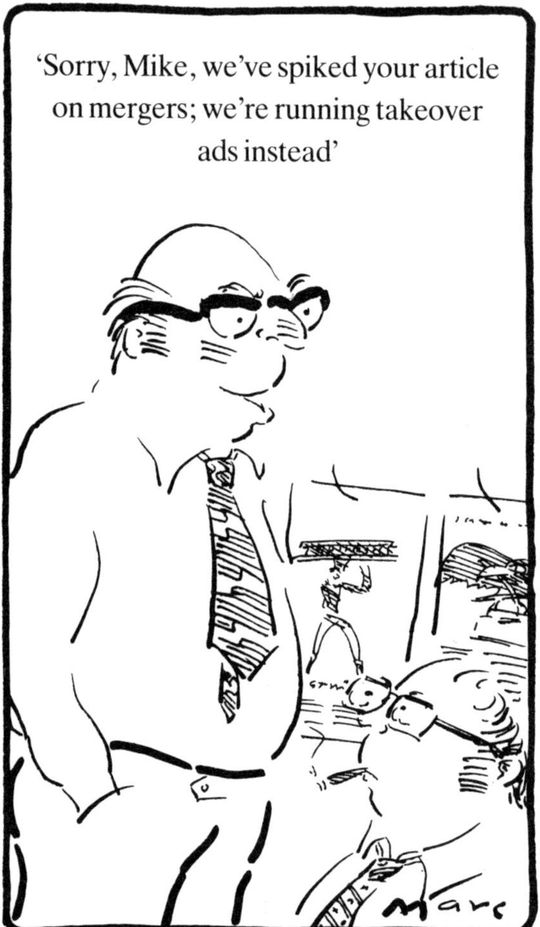

'Sorry, Mike, we've spiked your article on mergers; we're running takeover ads instead'

The Guardian February 6th 1986

'Yer, we've made this ace video. Next week we're gonna write the song'

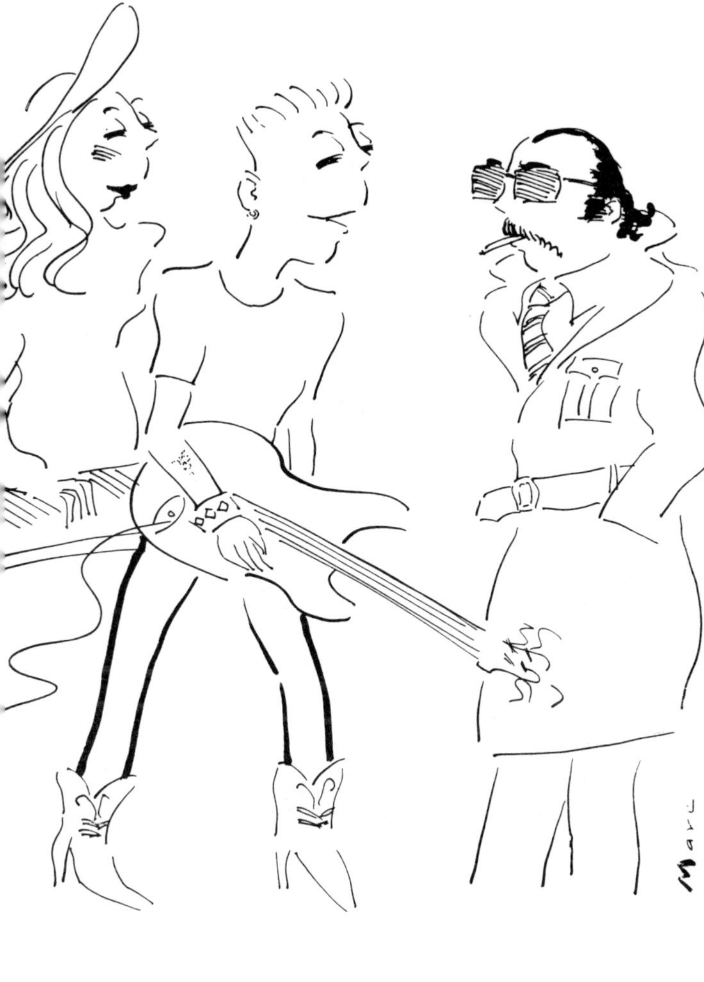

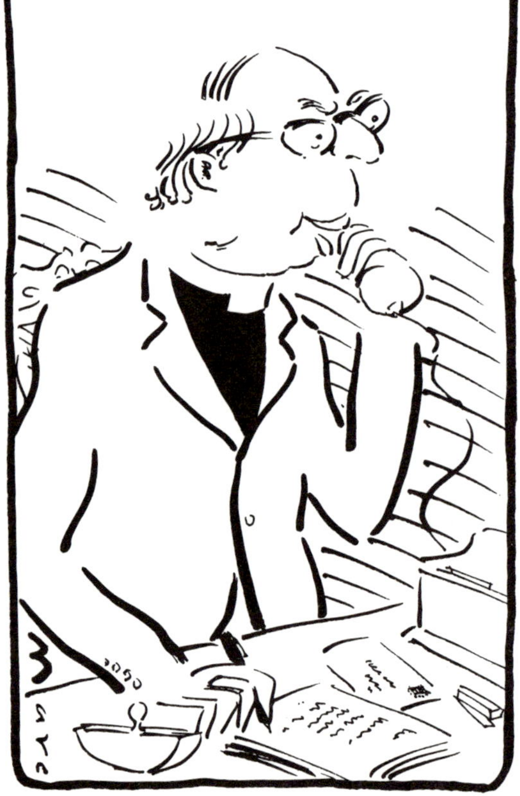

'Is that Securicor? I want you to deliver a letter to the Times...'

The Guardian February 5th 1986

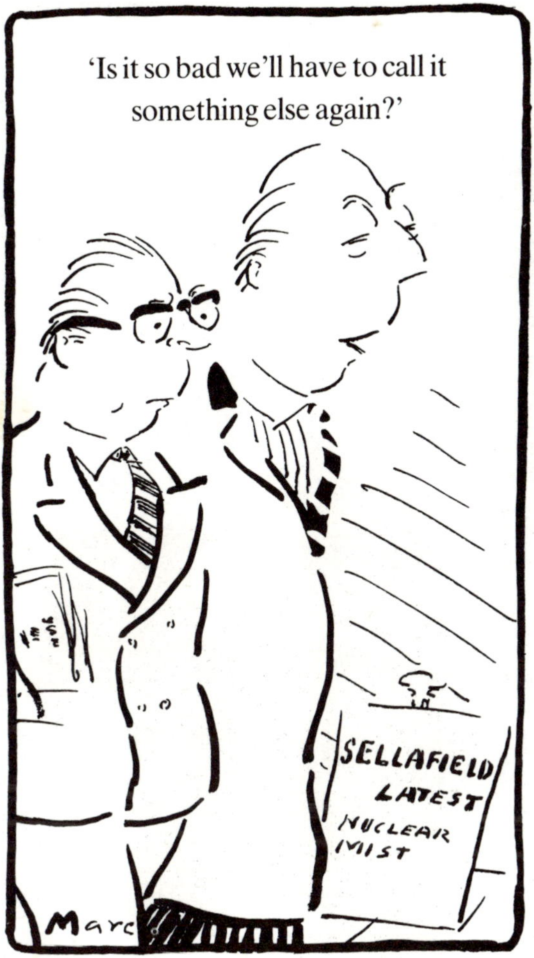

'Is it so bad we'll have to call it something else again?'

The Guardian February 7th 1986

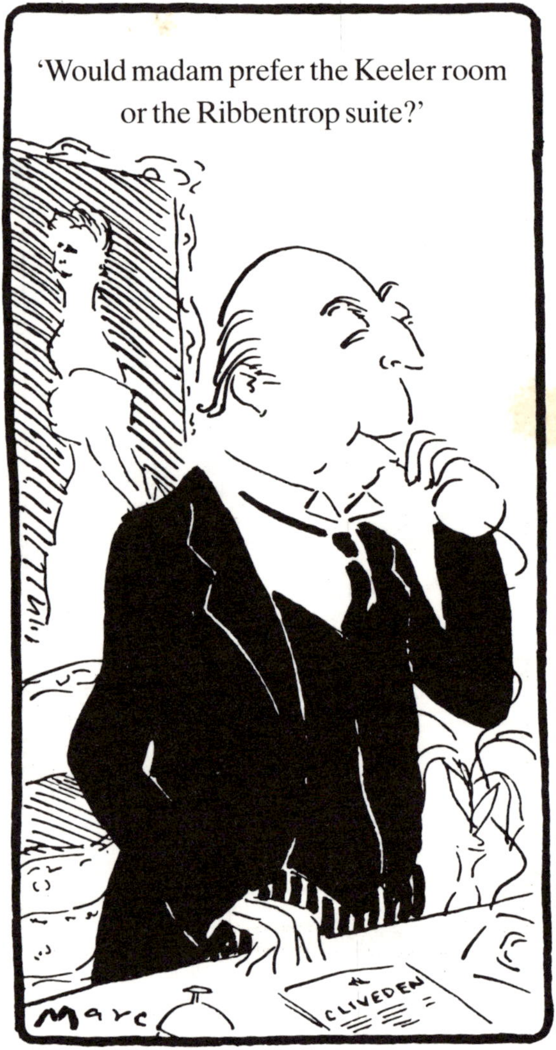

'Would madam prefer the Keeler room or the Ribbentrop suite?'

Cliveden opens as a hotel
The Guardian February 19th 1986

‘Is today’s leak from Sellafield or the Cabinet?’

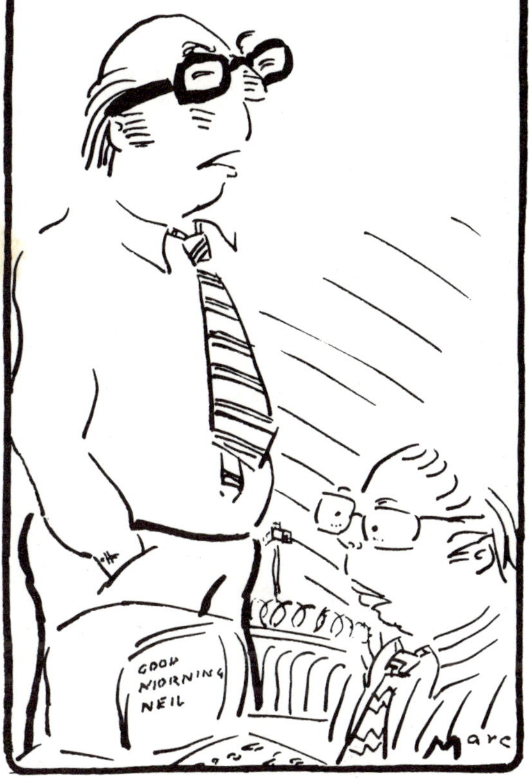

The Guardian February 20th 1986

‘Daddy’s worried we may have to go back to Portuguese servants’

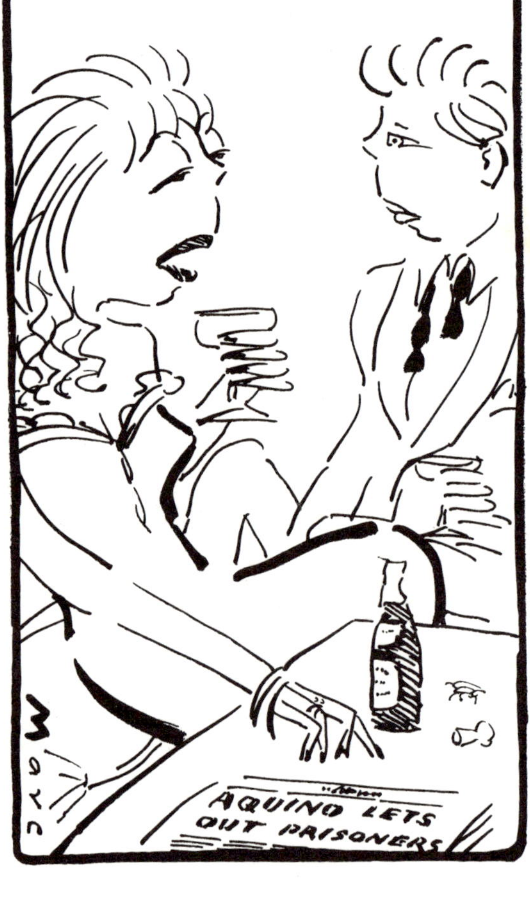

The Guardian March 4th 1986

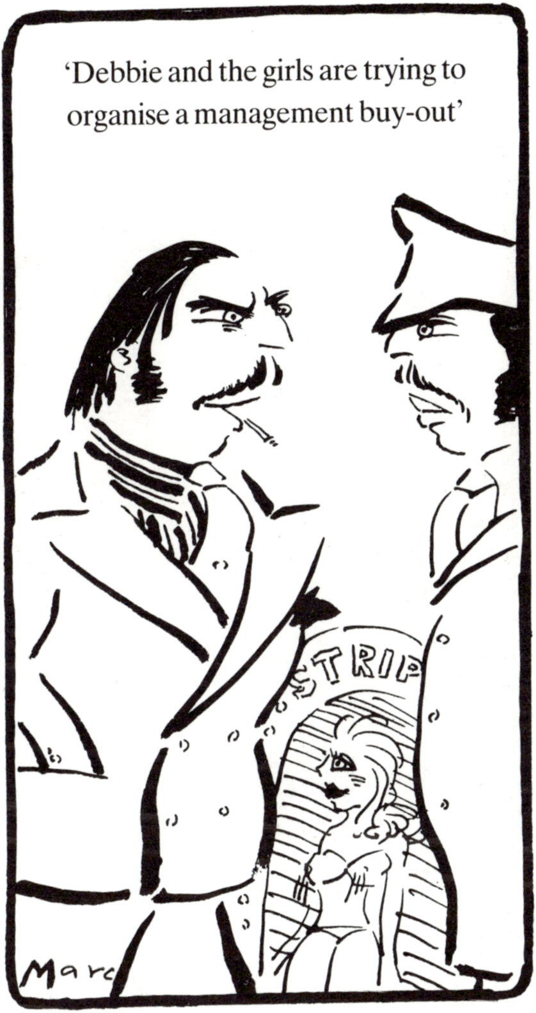

'Debbie and the girls are trying to organise a management buy-out'

The Guardian March 18th 1986

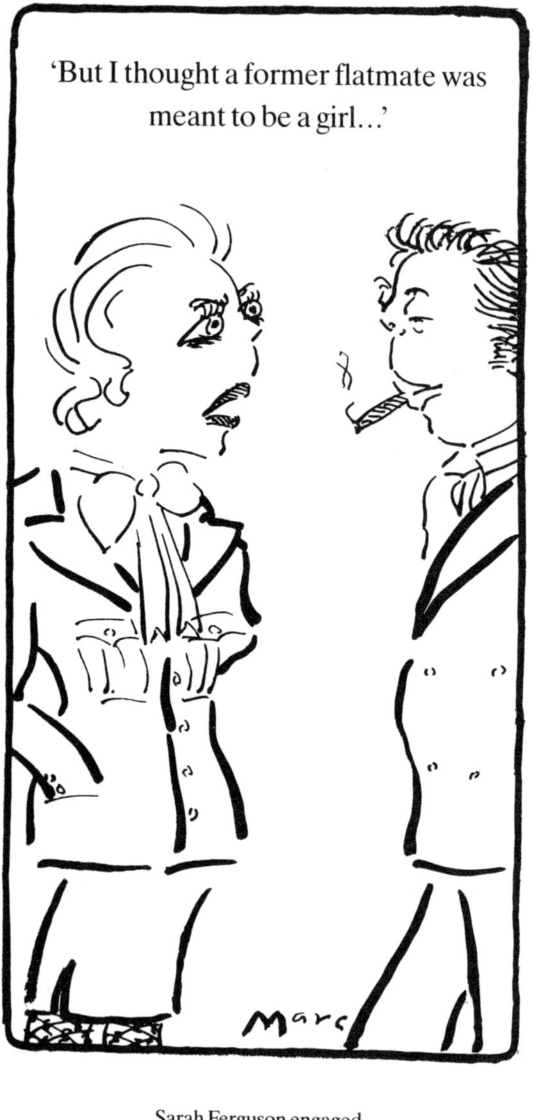

Sarah Ferguson engaged
The Guardian March 20th 1986

'My daughter is *so* conventional: she *said* she was spending the night with a girl friend and it came to light that she actually *was*'

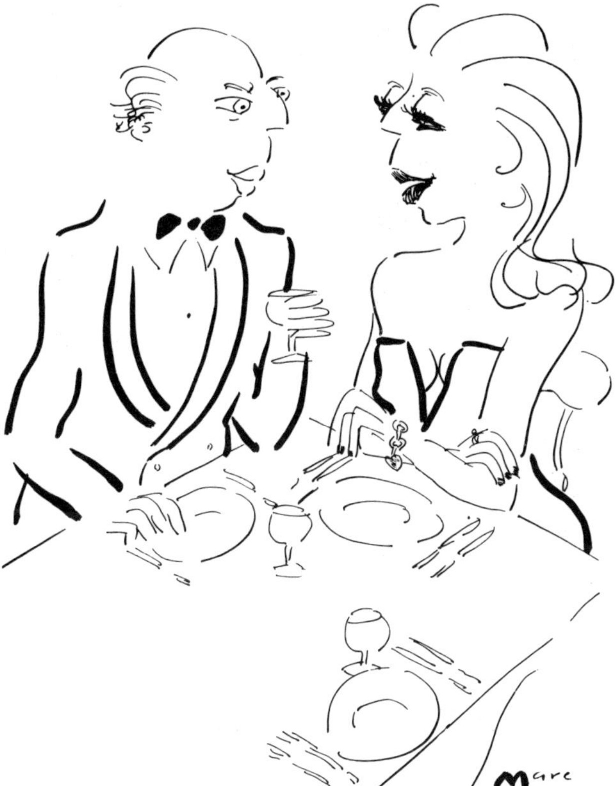

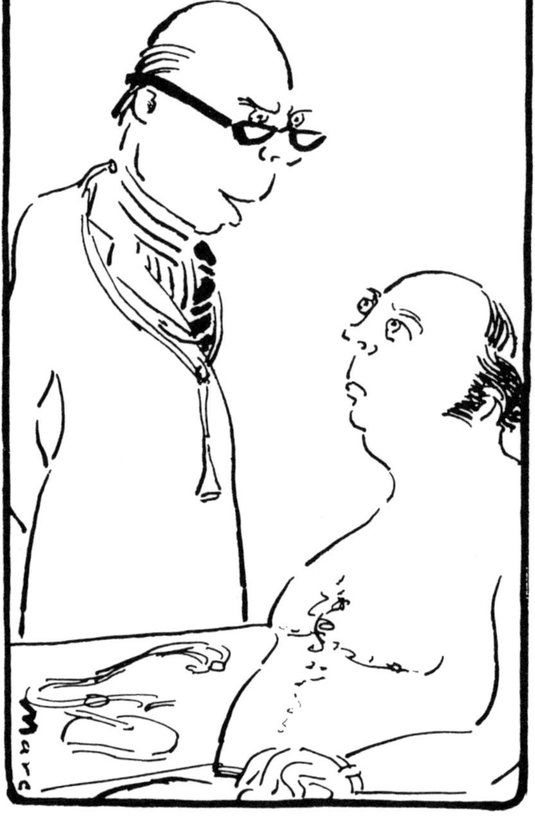

'You need more exercise: what about a walking holiday in Terminal 4?'

The Guardian April 3rd 1986

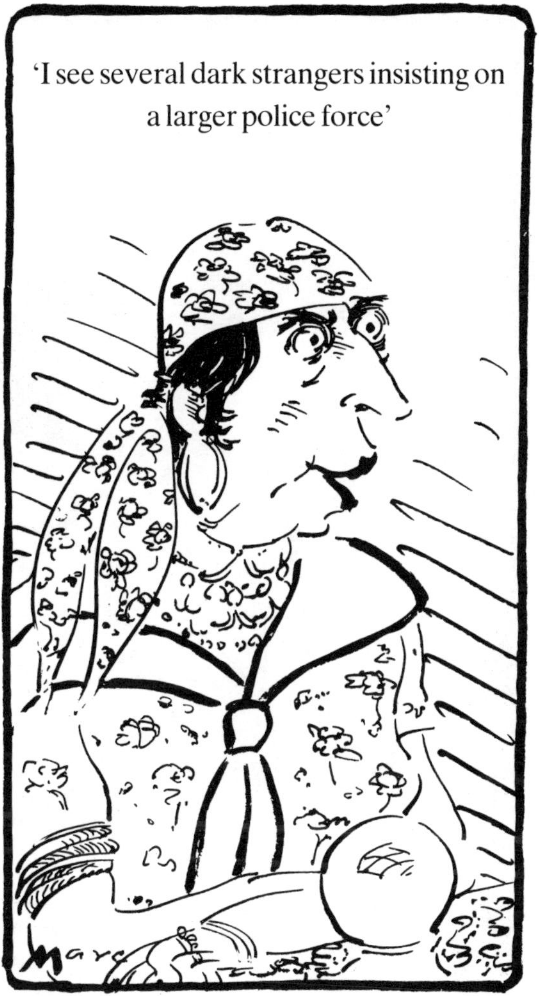

Police leaders request extra men
The Guardian May 23rd 1986

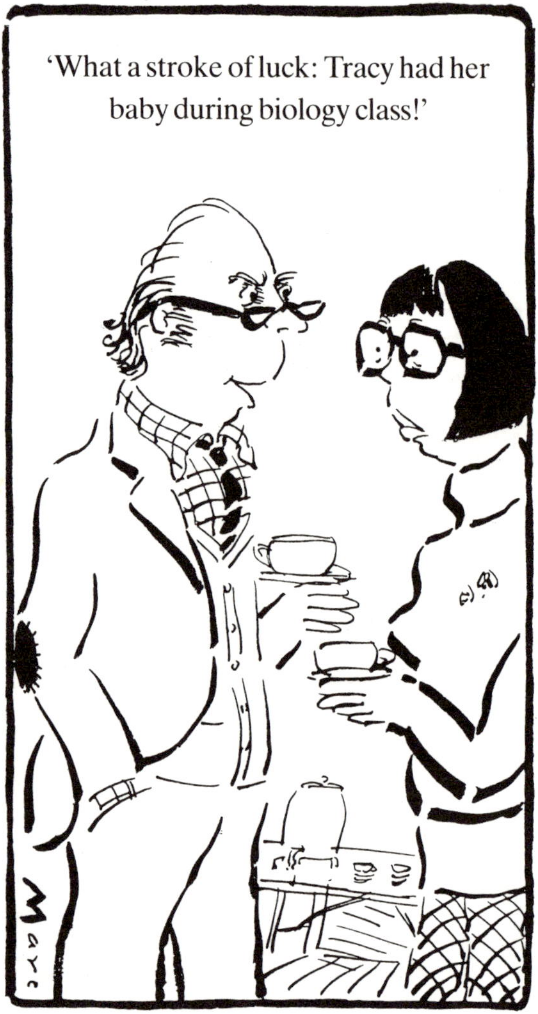

'What a stroke of luck: Tracy had her baby during biology class!'

Child born to child in class
The Guardian May 22nd 1986

'What's so brill about everyone being out of work is that they can all come to the wedding...'

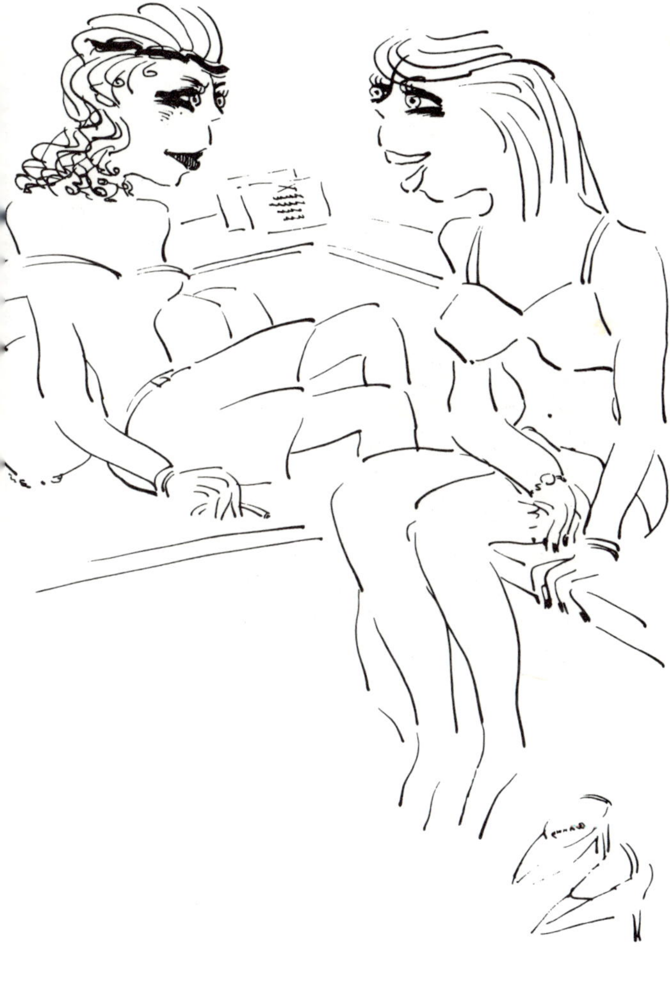

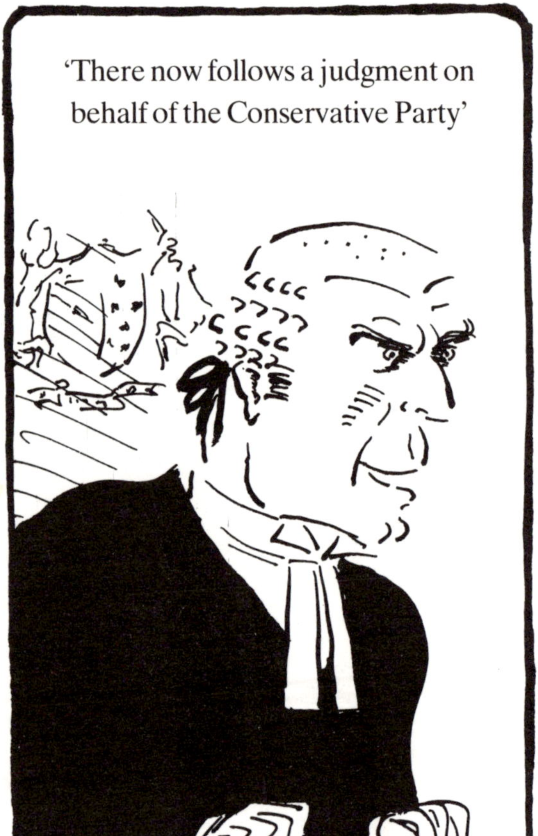

'There now follows a judgment on behalf of the Conservative Party'

The Guardian March 27th 1986

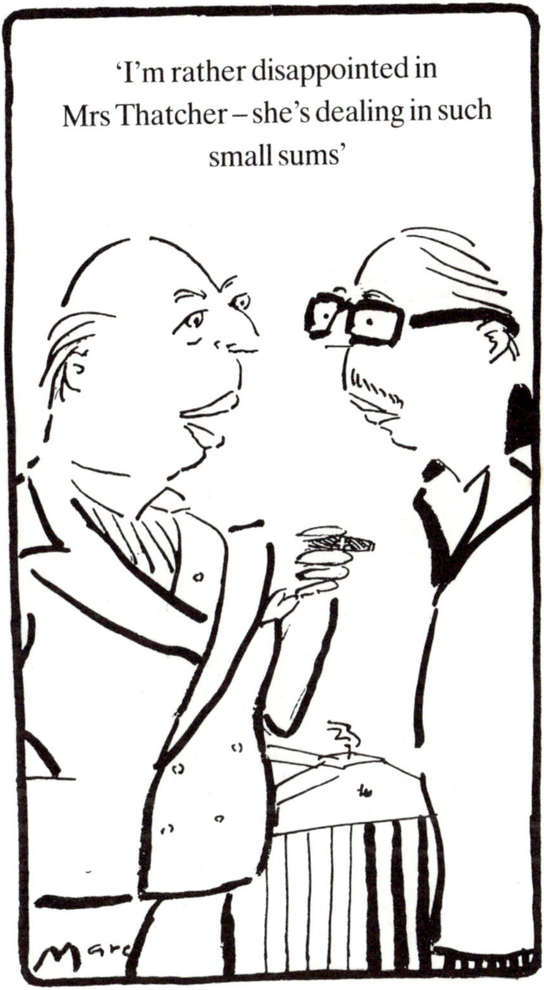

Mrs Thatcher's share dealings disclosed
March 1986

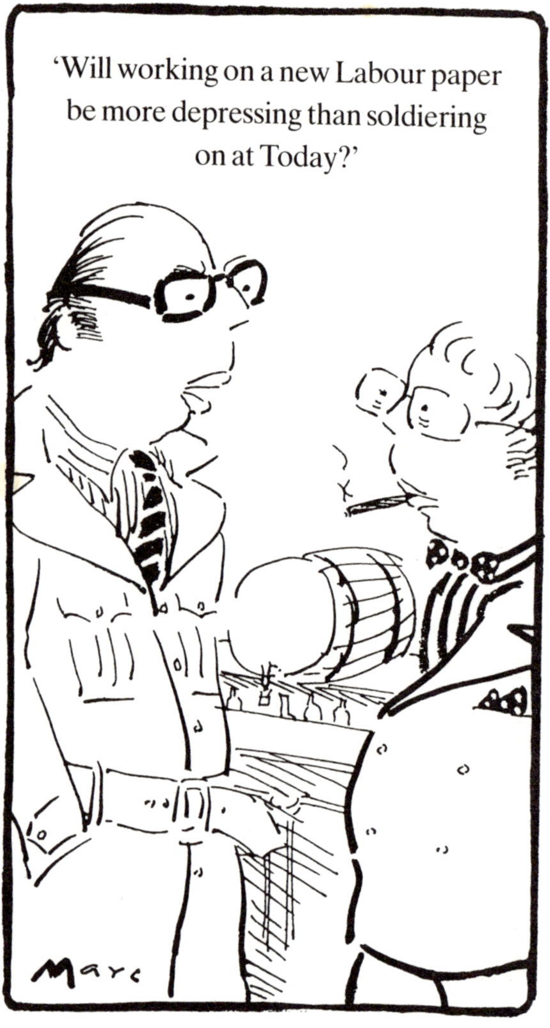

Today in trouble
April 1986

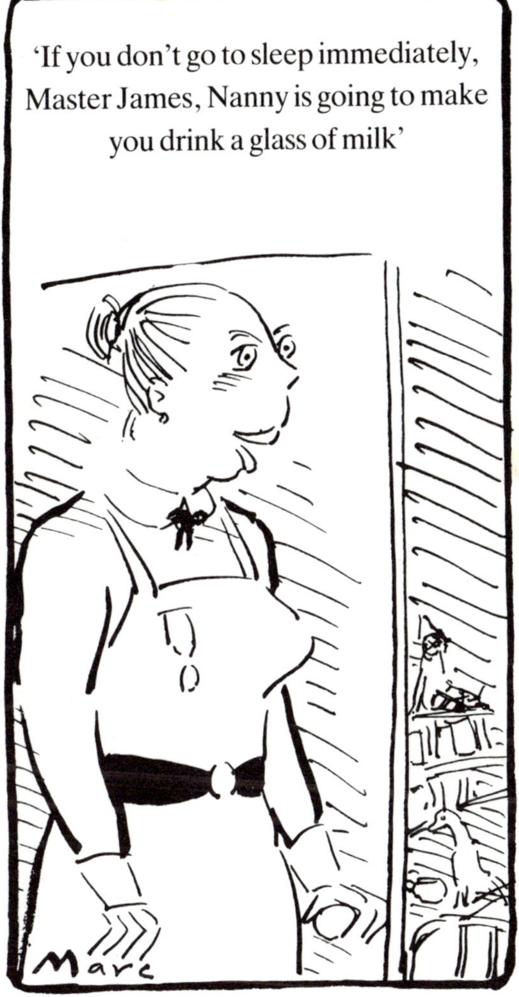

'If you don't go to sleep immediately, Master James, Nanny is going to make you drink a glass of milk'

Chernobyl
May 1986

‘Do you remember when politicians blamed everything going wrong on oil prices going *up*?’

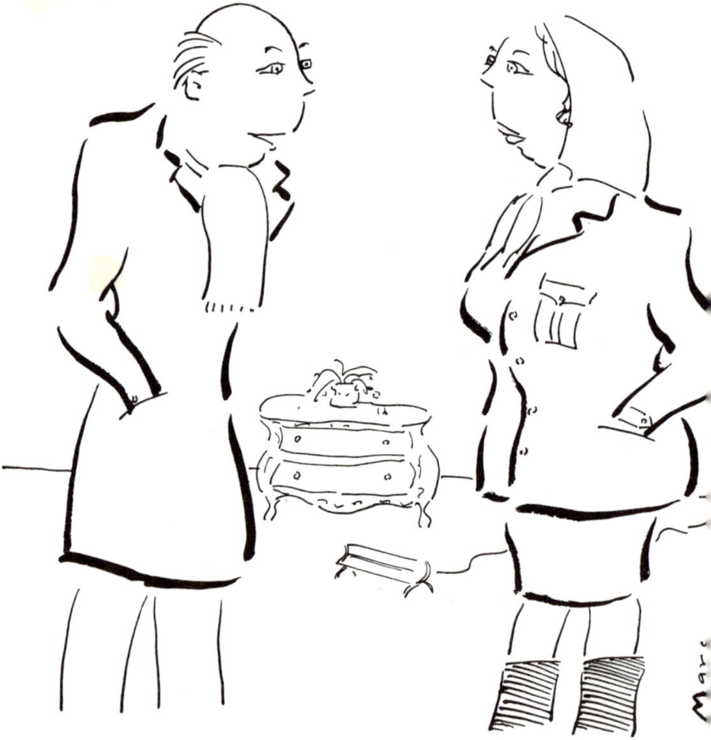